BX WRITERS ANTHOLOGY

VOL.1

EDITED BY: JOSUE CACERES
ART BY: AMAURYS GRULLON

Edited by: Josue Caceres
Art By: Amaurys Grullon
Blurb By: Anabel Encarnación
Bronx Native
BX Writers
127 Lincoln Ave
Bronx, NY 10454
josue@bronxnative.com
www.bronxnativeshop.com

Thank you to Leonardo Castillo for your generous support and
encouragement.
Leonardo Castillo Instagram- @cloudl30

Thank you to Anabel Encarnación for your inspiration and
encouragement behind the titling of this book.

CONTENTS

PRESENTS:

BX WRITERS ANTHOLOGY

VOL.1

EDITED BY: JOSUE CACERES
ART BY: AMAURYS GRULLON

ANABEL ENCARNACIÓN
Introduction

I met Josué on the day he released his second book, Bronx Stories and Heartbreak. We immediately bonded over a mutual love for the words and the Bronx. Soon we became friends, and over nachos and Modelo Negras at the Mott Haven Bar and Grill, right around the corner of the Bronx Native shop, we'd discuss mutual ideas. Ideas of the past that manifest in the present, as well as personal and community goals for both the near and distant future.

We'd pick on each other's brains to figure out what is it that we are doing-- to figure out our purpose. This was a question that we constantly ask ourselves due to our innate need to help others, even before helping ourselves. Endlessly, we'd string our ideas together—a linear and extensive quilt of ideas. It was a mutual love of poetry and the Bronx that drove us to each other, but it was our mutual need to create that continues to bond our friendship.

Through his words, Josué connects with others. As a self-published poet, Josué constantly reflects on the creation of his personal platform to share his poetry with others. As a NYC teacher, I constantly reflect on how my students are often rarely given the educational platform to advocate for themselves-- to write for themselves, to think for themselves. In both of our vocations we found that those that we interact with could benefit from the creation of a collective space where they feel heard, seen and felt.

And so finally, half way through are usual chicken nachos, and perhaps one too many Modelo Negras, Josué looked at me, with the wild look he gets when he has a dope idea. He then uttered four syllables that marked the genesis of this project anthology: BX Writers.

BX Writers is about shedding light on all things Bronx, and thus the BX Writers platform was created-- for Bronx people by Bronx people. This platform was about creating a space where Bronx-born or raised writers could present the thoughts that often lived in the vicinity of their notebooks and journals. We've even come to notice that these thoughts often do not even make onto paper. They stay confined in brains too afraid to transmit these words through a pen and eventually onto paper. Or in the case of our digital writers, these thoughts do not get to rush through our tapping fingertips and into our screens. There are a plethora of reasons why words often feel more comfortable within the confines of our expansive minds, but BX Writers is Josue's genuine attempt to create a virtual and metaphysical environment for people to take on their identities as writers.

An identity that often seems more than just far, but impossible, for there is this false narrative that the Bronx is still burning. We are not burning, we carry the fire within us. And so when these words, that burn in our minds ingrained, finally find a platform, they stand out like a million suns. All equally bright. All equally fire.

The written works featured in this first anthology includes a collection of poems, short stories and narratives predominantly from people in the Bronx. The writers in this anthology explore a plethora of themes, that include, but are not limited to identity, pride, love, community, loss, and anxiety… These works explore the daily lives of writers as they walk and breathe in the streets of the Bronx, and New York City in general. Through their work they explore the many lessons they learned in the schools that are Bronx and overall NYC streets. They write about the often gritty yet transcending experience of growing up and living in the Bronx.

This anthology aims to shed light on the things that you can only learn while being here. There are lessons that one can only learn while being in the borough(s). We learn not only to distrust the MTA and the weather, but also to adapt simultaneously to different situations. For here it is possible for the sky to cry and smile simultaneously. Some of us learn to create and foster certain identities depending on the social context, while others of us work to create one single identity that is unbothered by the sidewalk side eyes we may receive. Nevertheless, one thing remains constant: these streets shape our social and psychological identities. As the Ubuntu proverb goes: I am because you are. And in this context, we are because the Bronx is.

And while there are words that only exist within the perimeter of our minds, words that live only within those boundaries, this anthology is for those whom were brave enough to give those words a home beyond the confounds of their mind.

On behalf of the writers featured in this anthology, and the future readers, I'd like to thank Josué for his own courage. For creating BX Writers and providing our borough's unsung voices with a platform.

Without further ado, here it is, the first independently published Bronx anthology, by and for the people of the Bronx, and our sister boroughs— this is BX Writers.

JOSUÉ CACERES
you know where I'm from?

I'm from a place
where we witnessed the birth of culture
where vultures try to erase and displace
Concrete jungle
where the train never comes
It's either SHOWTIME!
or the sound of the drums

I'm from a place
where guys spit their first rhymes
Where they tell you make it out the hood
or resort to crime
Where you sleep to the sound
of sirens and cops
where you hang at bodegas and barbershops
Where growing up you'll get jumped
and they'll leave with your phone
Where la vecina is the nights-watch
and mami is up 'til you home

I'm from a place
of durags and putting timbs to the floor
Where a dollar
got you an entire meal from the store
Where rent is high
the man says you gotta pay
Where mothers working 3 jobs
so their kids could eat another day

I'm from a place
where we lost many brothers
But we don't mind your stereotype
because we look out for one another

I'm from a place
that was burnt
and bridges built over heads
Where the man wants to gentrify the hood
but the idea is getting torn into shreds

Where the kids is playing
hydrant spraying
MTA I ain't paying
grandma praying

So get out the hood
'cus my radio is always playing
and yeah these bullets straying
but I love The Bronx
so I'll be staying

SILVIA MORALES
On the 6

sometimes sitting across from a subway writer
perhaps young poet who will surpass us
due to fearlessness
discipline
and a habit more regular
than the train schedule
sitting somewhat apart
in spite of this rush-hour crowd
next to a student highlighting text
a bible reader
sports enthusiast to her left
and a hip hopper standing by the door
looking over her shoulder

At Parkchester she has filled two pages
is having trouble with her pen

By Hunts Point she has filled three more
now ink like a dark wound on her left wrist

At 138th she is like the train

gathering speed

no longer describing a dream

or recalling a memoir

but flashing quickly into the future like the lights going by

her 5 x 8 notebook is new

hardbound

tropical print fabric cover

surely a gift

from an admirer

at 125th Street I get up to transfer and look

to see that her writing is small

neat and most likely

painfully

cuttingly

precise

Silvia Morales

How to Cross the Grand Concourse

The Concourse
you got to take it one island at a time
aka meridian, boulevard, or median strip
whether you're crossing from east to west
or west to east
to visit your friend
or going home
you want to get there alive
with the strawberry swirl
so

you can cross at the corner
and let the berries thaw
and the cream melt
or you can take it one island at a time

you're in a hurry
to see your love
so you cross in the middle

look	if you see
no cars	jump
to the other side	

try not to lose your contact
lenses

now's the dangerous part
when all is gray wasteland
hurry across   try to look cool

if you crossed at the corner
oh patient and wise
the lights will become impatient
when you're only halfway across
don't let the honks make you   jump
stand your ground
it's against the law for them   to squash you
flat

even if you move like Bolt
the wheelestrians
like to honk   make you jump
then they laugh
be cool   don't jump
if you jump   you still have
options
ask God to forgive them

give them the finger ask God to
forgive you

the Concourse you got to take it one
island at a timc

now you're almost there use your
superhuman
vision no cars comin'

from behind that U-Haul truck? book it

now you made it praise the Lord
now you know how to cross
the grand concourse

SALLY FAMILIA

181st, Washington Heights

The bible

La habichuela con dulce

The bodega

The radio

Los aguacates

The shopping cart

The theater

La secadora

The hookah

The Presidente

Good Friday

You say that the end is near.
That we should surrender to Him.
That repentance
but your voice drowns amid the merengue
playing on the radio by the table of purses.

Brown skinned lady,
que dulce eres.
I hear them pleading for you.
I imagine you
breathless. Burned fingers intertwine with each other.
Gratitude spills over the sides of your mouth.

The bodega cat inspects the floor.
He smells the cuffs of my jeans for reassurance,
then continues to guard the beans.
If I were a cat, I'd stay here too.
Goya beans and cassava convert
into something beautiful at least once a year.

Sally Familia

After Five Mojitos on a Monday

I am reminded of the sun.
The delicate sounds of the earth.
The crunch of an auburn colored leaf.
The secret language of hummingbirds.

I am reminded of the moon.
How it appears brighter during a forest fire.
How it manages to control tides but still shy away from lava.

I am reminded of the stench of nameless trees.
The redness of them all.
The swift motions of the flames.
Like a flamenco dancer, a flower rests still upon the body.
She listens for the patterns of the earth.

The melodic tones of Caribbean rain on rusted sheet metal
ceilings.
The rocking chair moved by a gust of wind.
The muddy footsteps of a five-year-old girl.

Darriel McBride
The Hustle

Some say
the hustle runs through our veins.
Nah, fam.
We *are* the hustle.

Our moms would give us $1 and say,
buy something for everybody.

As youth,
we learn how the struggle
is its own dance.
Whether graceful or painful,
there's beauty in it all.

So we milly rock on any block
through the mud,
the sunshine,
& rain
while bumping Tupac
& Biggie classics

like it's the national anthem.

The concrete jungle
is an army of ghetto kids
forced to grow up too fast.
Half-empty stomachs
& calloused hands,
we feel and see everything
while carrying the weight
of the world on our backs.

We eat hate speech
with grit and swag
then spit it back out,
with our unrefined hip hop
& spoken word poems.

We refuse
to let our guard down
because our priority
is survival.

But what they don't teach us

is that the only way to beat the streets

is to radiate self-love,

until nothing can break us.

Darriel McBride

Street Anxiety

My anxiety comes to me in the voices
and images of my ancestors.
They flow through my veins
in twists and turns
on this horrid roller coaster
called democracy.
My anxiety comes to me
in the knot in my stomach
or that lump in the back of my throat
as I confess these things
that most will never believe.

Sometimes,
my anxiety comes to me in miraculous tears
triggered by the millions of black and brown bodies
that have been ripped and dragged through history.

Sometimes,
my anxiety comes to me in a nightmare
of my body covered in bullet wounds.
My body left laying on this soil

that belongs to none of us
until the wind carries my off bones,
and the rain white washes away the evidence.

And sometimes,
my anxiety turns into
a repressed ghetto rage
because life often feels like
a social experiment
that we have no place in
except as the subject.
Objects.
Moved in parts
& discarded when necessary.

I feel so irrelevant.
Yet, they always come for the great ones.
The ones that say too much
And write poems like this,
that never win poetry competitions
because they say suffering
is somehow
too political to publish.

Darriel McBride

Ain't I Latina?

No, I don't speak spanish,
but I can roll my rs
and still pronounce, *Yo soy boricua*
with a certain level of pride.

No, I don't speak spanish,
but if I wanted to
I could cook a mean
plate of arroz con habichuelas y pollo.

No, I don't speak spanish,
but my mother will still
hit us with a chancleta
whenever she needs to.

No, I don't speak spanish,
but my favorite food growing up
was always mi abuela's.

No, I don't speak spanish,
but after school,
you could always find me

Darriel McBride

at the cuchifrito.

No, I don't speak spanish,
but Taino blood still
bumps through my veins.

No, I don't speak spanish,
but I've got brown skin
and curly hair
that most wish they had.

No, I don't speak spanish,
but the beat of the conga
is in perfect harmony with my heart.

No, I don't speak spanish,
but I can teach you
how to dance salsa,
bachata, and merengue.

No, I don't speak spanish,
but I know enough
about my culture
to explain it to you.

No, I don't speak spanish,
but I didn't know I needed it
to feel the rhythm of our music
that ignites my internal fire.

I didn't know I needed it
to feel the brutal hands
of oppression that we endure.

No, I don't speak spanish
and that's alright.
My ancestors
didn't speak it either
before they were colonized.

CARLOS ERNESTO MATIAS
Six-Word Stories From The Bronx

"Mom, firecrackers!" "No, get down, baby"

Boy becomes man. Man becomes hashtag.

He shoots! Game over. They shoot.

No one could save the hero.

Store closing. Coming soon: Luxury housing.

"Welcome home, officer," tapping the coffin.

Soldier saves lives, except his own.

Went to school. Never went home.

"Call a doctor!" yelled the doctor.

A home run helped America heal.

Trip to store. Paid with life.

Portrait of boy on building wall.

FRANCHESCA PEÑA
Summer 2018

I swear if it was me, I'd kill every one of their families.

Venom sputters off our lips onto the next, like we each only
six degrees away from death.
But when the threats and blows come and go, all we got left is
this blood on the streets.
When the reporters and celebrities come and go, and the
weeks come and go, all we got left
are colors on pavement where the candles used to be.

I swear, let it have been me...

You want us to speak in extremes, like the hood don't hug us
and cut us. They want us to
speak in singularities, like the hood don't speak to us in
truths. How can we tell you we fear
for our kids. And yes, sometimes we fear our kids. When
you'll go and round them up like
they ain't kids.

I swear if it was me, I'd get them all outta there and move some nice people in.

And all there'll be left are the names of the slain on street signs of where we used to live.

Franchesca Peña

Justice Sought

We are due a justice that is not soaked in blood,
that memorials and obituaries aren't a part of.
That does not require rallies, and protests, and marches.
Give us a justice that we are not tired of.
A justice that is not collateral.
That is not temporary leave. Temporary paid leave.
Fire the guilty. We want consequences.

We want a justice that knows that men are not just bones and
women just skin. That knows we are all the same on the inside
expect when our insides are spilling out. And blood is not
just blood. Not when it is on the ground or in our hands.

We demand a justice that demands itself.
Tired of loose shells and loose spines.
Bending backwards cowards.
Don't you know what it is to be killed?
Aren't you alive?

Bronx Beauty Queen

I find a beauty supply in every neighborhood I go to.
Watch the neighbors when they watch me to see if I could:
knock the consonants out my mouth,
let my lips loose,
this my hood too.

I find a sunset on every block that I'm on.
Watch the sky turn blue and heavy like the ocean,
I hear wind in palm trees that ain't even there.
Find green residue on my hands and behind my ears
from 100% sterling silver.
Still spend my paychecks on hoops.
Make home wherever I go,
Could even make one out of you.

Adorn this body with 4.99 jewelry,
cause home is me.

I check myself out in a store display
before a man comes and gets in the way.
I went to Paris once.
This guy said I don't even look like a tourist;

Said he liked my head-wrap.

Dinner?

He knew a place.

W i n e a n d c h e e s e- Men ain't shit.

Got naked hands but I know the smell of acrylic.

Suck my teeth to taste saliva sticky with memories:

I always look for a mirror.

Always find my reflection.

Daily reminder that a bitch is still standing.

GRETCHEN GOMEZ

some train stops away from the x

i'm a few train stops away from non-existence

and when i get off this train stop

my body is now a political party

it is the revolution you didn't want

it does not fit your 5th Avenue confinement

i open my mouth and they hear accent

they hear 2nd class citizen

mothers screaming from the 5th floor

they hear welfare

they got me second guessing the movement of my hands

the tapping of my acrylic nails

how i placed my curly hair all to the left side of my face to

give it more bounce

that's exactly what i do

i bounce

i ride the train home

and feel more at ease when i see people come in who look

like me

my body relaxes when the train stops to similarity

more like family

what is othering if we all walk the same way

Gretchen Gomez

talk with hands that always have something to say
understanding that we fight the same struggle every day
in the bronx my body is not a democracy
it is a god given talent
in the bronx when they hear my accent
they hear angels being sent to help
we see equality

Gretchen Gomez

entierro de pobre

when things are going fast
mami loves to say esto va como enterrio de pobre

pobre
survival

these two should be synonyms
what is time
there is no mourning
survival must go on

mami cleans the house quickly
before papi comes home from work
cuando tu pai venga del trabajo,
vete rápido pal cuarto

i walk down the street and see them
doing their graffiti on the walls
fast
before the cops come

i ask the bodega man if he can make

me coffee quick cause i'm about to
lose my train

and i see all of us
fast life livin'
overcoming our troubles on the go
cause there is no privilege of time
given to us on these pobre streets

Gretchen Gomez

i dream of love

i dream of love
wild love
the love that cannot harbor me
provoke every fiber of my being
to be more
more than i already am
i dream of love
it's embrace
the fire
one whole being
all self
singing in the kitchen
full accepting of my madness
my laughter and my cries
i dream of love
in our language
calling me mi amor
sweet like mangoes
screaming out the window of a car
unfiltered and full of rebellion
i dream of love
the way a hopeless romantic watches novelas

Gretchen Gomez

with their dramatics and happy endings

knowingly wanting it

full fledged hearted

i dream of love

but it never comes

AJAY RAM

on friendship and being the lesser of twins

dear kindred,

ever since I was a kid, I've wanted to be like you. long before I
even met you, you were the woman I dreamed of becoming;
the spitting image of my third grade aspirations of being
graceful and fashionable and stunning and funny but in a
chill way and not an erratic one. I was a boy with biracial
brillo textured hair and two left feet and I hated me. I wanted
to be you. warm and magnetic and feminine and tall and
sporty. masculinity is so heavy, especially as a child with no
father figure to provide a mirror for my imposed identity. it
bruised my spine and twisted my posture and I've never really
wanted to be a boy. my voice never situated into it's bass. it
cracks alot, but truthfully, it's more like it's glitching. my room
feels like a womb for the wrong fetus, and yours felt like a
repass for all the truth I could have lived in. in your bed, I
became acquainted with stability for the first time, and when
February first hit, the realization that I couldn't stay hit me
like a landslide. the reality that fracture is my norm. that
confusion is my homeostasis. that I've been wired to short
circuit like an outlet in a hurricane. when I washed your

sheets and pillows the night before I left, I felt like I was finally nurturing myself. I sat in the laundromat, staring at your red comforter in the spin cycle as though it was a newborn version of the baby I was 'spose to be birthed as. my long awaited wholeness was right in front of me in the dryer, and although I knew this moment would soon shuffle back into my fallible memory bank, I still soaked it in like time itself was a defunct concept.

a thesis: is what I feel in the most primordial corners of my soul correct? that I truly am two beings inhabiting one body; the (feminine) one I yearn to fully embrace being lost in the fire decades ago and the (masculine) body I'm left to stumble around within ? or am I just schizophrenic? I've never felt like an only child. I felt like my other half was always in the room with me, in a state of agonizing intangibility. she was lost, both within me and without a body of her own. I am her, but also, she is her, and her "death" in the womb twenty-six years ago robbed her of the autonomy she truly deserved.

I want her to feel the sunshine on her face.
I want her to be free.
and my fear of the truth is her burial.

the soil I stand on wants me dead. the bed I sleep in wants to take me under like quicksand. I'm black. I'm brown. I'm queer. I'm terrified. my daily existence is confusing to say the least, maddening to say more.

I'm melting.
I'm shattering.
I'm breaking laws of physics daily.

when the lights are restored after a spiritual blackout, do they shine a bit dimmer? much dimmer? can you read in them? dance? hold hands? or will the room still be too dark to do much of anything in? and what do you do when the oppressive system you need to separate from is… yourself? I dig to the core and find uranium where milk and honey should reside. where your childhood had the warmth of a bed, two parents, and close bonds from birth, mine had the open wounds of squalor, divorce, and alienation. you have fond memories, while I'm haunted by grisly flashbacks. you levitate. I drown in mid-air.

between the two of us, I'm the lesser of twins.

KEVA G

Amerikkka

I have been gagged by the constitution

blindfolded by the American flag

lynched by my box braids

I hang with niggas that shuck/jive for a higher spot

On the tree

'cuz if we gonna die

We die with the oppressors apologies on our lips as they
tighten our nooses

And be proud

When they watch our bodies sway in the wind

"Look massa! See how my neck twists for you?"

This isn't a black poem

I do not want to label anything

Black

For fear it will be taken from me

Gentrified

then returned on a Styrofoam plate

This is the cycle of black things

They are born

Drenched in flour

Turned into a hashtag

Distorted to fit the "All lives Matter" agenda:

"Well black people didn't invent

(insert style/dance/talent here)"

Please do not label this as a black poem

I want this one

to keep

I do not need this poem remixed

into an acoustic version

Ain't no fun

Ain't not fun in being "woke"
When niggas ask you how your day was
You confuse your day with that of those
Buried under the jail for a dime bag
And the blunt start to hit differently
Like this feeling of euphoria does not belong to you
Like your freedom does not belong to you

Ain't no fun in being "woke"
You know college is a scam
And you see your momma struggling to pay your way for a
piece of paper
that probably won't get you hired anyway
Once they see how your name is spelled
But they don't care how its pronounced
Or where it comes from
Just like that
Your lineage as a CEO is snuffed out before it even began

Ain't no fun in being "woke"
Anyone who says that is a liar looking for brownie points
But we don't give awards for who can suffer the most...

Keva G

Unless you're a poet

Unless you're sworn duty on this earth is to peel away at
yourself until all that is left is suffering
My bones used as wind-chimes on a mogul's porch
Do they sing softly to you?
Or do they scream war songs so loud you don't ever wanna
visit the hood again?

Being "woke"
It is not a badge of honor
It is realizing that everything about yourself must be ripped
away and built back up by no one other than yourself
Being "woke" makes you lose friends and family
Because who got time to teach those who don't wanna be
taught?
Being "woke"
Is facing down the barrel of society's gun
And everyday you wake up
Is a new round of Russian roulette

I stare death in the face everyday
I wish that nigga would take me before my time!

Being revolutionary does not require anything else but the
drive to see change
And be change
I don't care how many times you've read
The Autobiography of Malcolm X
If you ain't practicing what the preacher teach
the whole congregation goes under

So no
It's not fun to be woke
But neither is being enslaved.

ANDREW TORRES

Lessons Learned in Retrospect

You look so familiar like seeing Ma in the kitchen whippin up
adobo miracles
Like saying Bendicion and hearing Dios te Bendigas
Like toasted butter bagels, hot chocolates,
And Tekken arcades after Children's Liberation on St. Marks
Place
Like blowing on Nintendo game cartridges
to get them to work
Like trying to be Michael Jackson with a fedora
And moonwalking in socks across shellacked hardwood

The rough contours of your silhouette reminiscent of starless
street nights
Voices of lyrical alchemists like Lavoe, Lauryn, and Pun
echoing off 5 story walk ups
The air smelling of loosies and Colt 45 gunpowder
Demonized souls drifting up and down the block
Like ghosts in the wind immortalized on the corner of worn
brick rooftops
Yet you look so familiar

Andrew Torres

Like seeing your step-father put money in Philly blunts boxes
stashed under the bed
Or feeling Mom's tears rain dropping on to your forehead as
she hid from his rage

Looking at you brings back memories of M-80 booms in the
middle of those humid summer nights around the 4th of July
Waking up in the dark morning hours when all is silent to
watch Ren and Stimpy
because you gave up on your dreams
Slipping on ice while defrosting the driveway
so Pop can go to Walgreens
and get great grandma's prescription

But looking at you is also strange for some reason
Like having a sister who's 6 months older than you
Or seeing a broke Afro-Boriken Bronxite graduate from ivory
towers
founded by the same guy on the 100-dollar bill

Where is this strange feeling from?

Is it from being bullied for breaking slave mentalities because
smart can never be cool?

Maybe it's from hiding a 1.4 GPA from shaming el orgullo de
la familia that first semester at Bing
It could be from not being claimed by daddy-daddy those
first five years
Either way it is hard to get over how familiar you look

Like seeing hoodies and Jordans turn to suits and pencil skirts
when you pass 96th street on the 6 train
Like that heart racing fear every time you get pulled over by
the cops
Like watching the L.E.S. being gentrified over the span of
your life time
Like la bandera puertorriqueña waving over 116th in El Barrio
Or the Apollo lighting up 125th in Harlem

Every detail of you engenders a sense of nostalgia deeply
rooted in this belief
that we know each other from way back

SONYI LOPEZ

Ode to Summers in The Bronx

Circa 97',

when cherry coquito

stained streets,

not blood.

Fire works,

not shots fired.

little girls were

Double-dutch dancers,

and boys

taunted and tagged.

they all came together

for fire hydrant baths.

neighbors necks out

ungated windows,

fire escapes.

we had to scream

a lil' louder

thru train

rumble and shakes.

Mister softee,

the hood anthem;

Sonyi Lopez

Kids
Merily
Merily
Hop & scotch,
And ring-around-a-pony.

Dollars stretched
on bodega trips,
Wise & Utz.
exclusive hood chips,
Pop rock lollipop foots,
sunflower seeds,
til' your mouth bleeds.

The moon brought
Bronx kids fun
to an end.

Here's to hoping the sun
summons summer to
the Bronx, again.

Sonyi Lopez

#JusticeforJunior

I pressed my fingers to my neck
and felt my pulse, today

Took a swig of water
and felt the gulp, today

Traced every single line in my hand
and felt the tingles, vein mountains and bones, today.

I stared at the sun,
squinted
And felt hope, today.

Mnemosyne

I remember grandma in her prime. Nails, always coated in lavender blankets. Hair, equal parts salt and pepper, curled behind her ear like snail shells. Her eyes, green Fibonacci spirals. Lips, left behind wet peachy pink prints on my cheek.

"Grandma! Why are your kisses so wet?" I'd say, scrubbing her lips off my face.

"Honey, save the dry lips for the dead!" She'd reply, smacking them together and kissing me again. Attempting to grab my face to apply shade #072, *peach perfection* on her apparently dead granddaughter's lips.

Grandma was my best friend. She was the most beautiful woman I knew, inside and out. I desperately look for her in every wrinkled face I see.

As grandma began to age, I thought I'd be afraid when I held her feeble hands, her over-ripe banana peel skin or when I looked into those cataract drowned islands eyes, or when I watched the frothy, snowy substance escape her lips as she convulsed in her bed. I thought I'd weep when she bruised upon tripping and falling down a flight of stairs. Or when she fell off her bed, trying to weasel her way out of the hospital, attempting to crawl back home. But none of those events were ever enough to break her, and so, they didn't break me.

I remember all of my nightmares dissipated with just my grandma's breath as she susurrate me to sleep.

"Grandma, can I sleep with you tonight?" I'd ask, standing at her bedside gripping my teddy and pillow. Breathless, after having dashed to her room outrunning the darkness of my own.

"You are old enough to sleep alone, honey. What do I always tell you when you're having a *pesadilla?*" She'd ask.

"Pray, grandma." I'd reply, while stealthy climbing onto her bed.

Grandma played with my hair and whispered to me, "That's right.. pray, *mi amor*. Get rid of the negative thoughts and just, pray."

It'd be the fourth time that week I attempted to escape the demons in my room. I'd drag myself back down the hallway, switch my room lights back on, and pray myself to sleep, the way grandma taught me.

Thank You Great Goddess for this day
for the blessings and lessons that came my way
May my sleep be peaceful in dreams and rest
and tomorrow, may I do my best.

She'd sneak in later to leave those peach lips on my face again, then she'd shut off the lights behind her and walk past the goddess' shrine in the hallway, between her room and mine. She'd whisper to the goddess', trickle water onto the flowers at the base and light a candle every night.

Slowly, my grandmother herself became those nightmares, that fateful day she forgot my name. She forgot who I was.

∞ ∞ ∞

Grandma began to forget things when I entered college at 19. Even though it was true she began to forget a lot of things, I was never afraid of her forgetting me. And so, every day I visited her at the hospital at noon, during my forty-five minute break between classes. I'd come back on Friday evenings and stay the night, through the weekend. I did it because I wanted to see her, of course. But also, because I didn't want her to ever forget me. It seemed she'd forgotten about all the things that no longer existed. But I was here, existing, by her side every day. But one Sunday, I no longer existed. Not in my grandma's mind, at least.

"Hey Grandma," I walked in the room, hanging my backpack on the door handle.

"Grandma, the flowers are dry, has that lady come in to water them today?, " I said.

She usually didn't answer me the first time around because she was either a. asleep or b. pretending to be asleep *so hard* that she actually fell asleep in an attempt to avoid the nurses. She'd rip her heart monitor off so they wouldn't sense the changes. Grandma hated nurses because they poked and prodded her. Sometimes, they even tied her to the bed because she'd get aggressive with them. Hell, injections every other day? Medicine in high dosages? I would get aggressive too. Despite all of that, grandma was still the sweetest to me when I came around.

"Grandma," I crawled into her bed, tickled her socked feet and tugged at her mumu.

She wouldn't move. I put my left hand on her chest and right hand under her nostrils. The silence of the room didn't permit me to hear any signs of life at first. But then I could feel her heart thuds, and breathing. I was relieved. I've had scares before, nurses running in to aid me because I couldn't feel her pulse. But by now, I'm an expert.

"Grandma, *levantate*, its 12:05. I have 35 minutes left!," I said.

She finally twitched a little. She opened her eyes and looked toward me.

"Hey, girl! ," I smiled.

She didn't return the greeting, or the smile. She didn't look me in my eyes. She didn't ask me how classes were so far today, or how the weather is outside. Nothing.

"Quien eres tu?," Grandma quivered.

She was afraid of me. I was a stranger at her bedside. A stranger tugging at her mumu and tickling her feet. She was pissed. And I was scared. I lost my breath for a minute, and regained it the next. I had enough breath in me to start speaking.

"Grandma, it's me..," I started.

"Nurse! ," She screamed.

I got up from her bed as her scream pierced through my heart. I looked at my grandma, I've never seen her this way. She gripped onto the bed sheets. Her eyes were turning crimson, her furrowing brows, and introverted laugh lines made her skin appear more wrinkled than ever. The nurses ran past me and tied her down as she kept fighting back as if resisting her memories of me.

I walked backwards, grabbed my backpack and felt as if my life was muted, and on rewind. Hoping tomorrow may be a better day, and all of this would be past us, I made my way down the hospital hall. I looked back and saw the flower watering woman enter my grandmother's room.

I returned the next day, and there she was. A sleeping beauty. When she woke up, she startled me. I flinched, expecting another scream, another horrid stare. But she just met my gaze and asked me to sit. So I did. After that day I became her new, nameless friend.

When the doctor's told she would *never* remember me, I tried praying at the shrine at home, but all I knew were sleep prayers. Those only worked to fend off nightmares, they couldn't make miracles happen for grandma. But I didn't lose faith. I lit that candle every night, I glued my hands together and mumbled a few words to the air. I tried rubbing *vivaporú* on her temples, in what I thought was an attempt to stimulate her mind, that stuff was a miracle growing up. If I had a cough, she'd slather it on my chest. If I stubbed my pinky toe for the 399th time, she'd coat it on. Those picture day pimples were saved by none other than *vivaporu*, the powerful all-use menthol ointment.

When I slathered it on her wrinkly temples, it just irritated her skin. If I made her sniff it, it made her sneeze. But I didn't know what else to do. I was helpless and hopeless.

"*Achoo!* Doctor! Crazy girl is in here torturing me with this stuff again," She'd yell.

"Abuela, it's just me, and its vivaporu! Not *stuff*," I'd respond.

The doctor never came, he knew the deal. Eventually, grandma gave into the crazy menthol lady and made her a friend all over again, every time.

A lovely, young woman, who I assumed was a volunteer, came into our room every Sunday carrying a gold stamna vase, to water the Anthuriums sitting atop of the desk near my grandmother's bedside. The young woman sauntered her way through the room, she used her white cane, drawing a path to the desk, like an Etch-A-Sketch. I knew she couldn't see me, but I also knew it was rude to stare. I'd never spoken to her before, but today, I needed to speak. I thought long and hard about what to say to her. I didn't want it to be awkward. I didn't want her to think I was speaking to someone else, grandma was asleep.

I sighed.

"She forgot my name." I finally said.

The woman seized her pouring. She turned to me. Her eyes were iris less clouds, they made my own eyes water. Her copper hair, the ends sinuous plumes, rested gently above her shoulders. She set the vase aside and continued to regard me.

"My grandmother, she for--"

"While it is true that I can only see a silhouette of you, it does not mean I do not know what mysteries the silhouette bears," she says.

I think I *offended* her.

"I'm awfully sorry if I've offended you, madam."

Awfully? Madam?.. really? Damn. I've adapted her
vernacular.

I snort at my own thoughts. A snot bubble pops out of
my nose.

"You haven't. Now, may I?" she says.

The woman summons me off the bed, away from
grandma and I stand idly beside her. She was a fortress of a
woman, me a peasant at her steps. Her shadow towers over
me as she glides closer towards my grandma. She draws her
hands in front of her and gently pats around until she finally
feels grandma's nose. Her hands sway a few centimeters down
to grandma's peachy lips. I've made it my mission to continue
lathering her favorite lipstick on them. I see the woman
moving her own lips, yet I can't make out what she's uttering,
the chime in her tone hints at prayer.

She snaps a yellow zinnia between her fingers and
tucks it behind my grandma's ear. I regard her now. The
clouds on the woman's eyes reveal the same green Fibonacci
spirals my grandma once had in her own eyes. I've seen her
before. In the hallway, in my home. I've looked into those
eyes, I've prayed to them. The clouds reform, she smiles
beautifully, then purses her lips and takes a step back. The

woman grabs her vase off the window sill, along with her white cane leaning against the wall. She begins to make her way out of the room.

"Wha-what is your name?" I ask her.

"You may call me Nemy," she replies, as she wiggles her white cane away from us.

"Your grandmother will be fine."

She has rendered me speechless. I am addled with the idea that this woman must've joined my grandma and me in this room one thousand times, yet, I never really noticed her. She was a stranger.

And now, *I know her*. I know her eye color beneath the fog matched my grandma's, I know she can snap healing flowers out of her fingertips.

Grandma swivels her neck around the room, like a fan on its lowest setting, she passes the IV machines, the steel commode, the Anthuriums, until she finally finds me at the corner of her bed. I meet her gaze. She lowers her eyes and with a thwarted smile, she regards my dry, desiccated lips.

"Hi, Grandma." I say, cracking the skin on my lips with a painfully big smile.

Grandma titters, "*Cielo*," She recites.

DESTINY PADILLA
Fuerte Hija

Fuerte Hija!

Como Abuela decía.

This strength I possess I once did not know where it
came from.
I am not dead yet, I thought.
I was moving like zombies,
breathing like vampires,
seeing only in black and white.

Voices and movements were in slow motion,
Driving backwards with no seatbelt on.
Both feet on the brake pressing down
as if it was the dirt I wanted to dig myself into for good.
The kind of dirt that caskets drop into.
Hoping my family remembers that sunflowers and roses
were my favorite.

People tried to help me.
Look! These pills, they can help you.

Destiny Padilla

Mr. Therapist can set you free
but really all they did
was hold up a mirror to my face.

I saw me for the first time,
my eyes begging for life,
my hair pulled back like Abuelas used to be,

She took over my reflection,
Dressed in white, we smiled at each other
And that's when I knew her dream visits
telling me to pray to my Ancestors were real.

My ancestors whisper into my ears
and tell me to stop lowering my voice.
I've accepted my Ancestors live inside of me
They are my divine compass, that set my soul free.

Nail files

My long fake nails
    help me
enjoy typing
for the corporate whites.
The neon polish
    helps me
believe, I brought
my friends to real
working girl life.
    the life
that Mami and Abuela
dreamed into my ears.
the reason they
    taught us,
that school
was the answer
to why we were
in
    this country.
why Puerto Rico,
was where I went for
    summers,

before

summer school was

needed so I

    wouldn't

have to repeat grades

seven through ten.

    my acrylic nails

claw the words,

"sell out"

    out of my

head, tongue and stomach.

I even stopped code

switching my voice

with my office mates,

    only.

When the big ones make

a stop in to stand

    over me,

I still

heighten my vocal cords

and curl my fingers

into my keyboard

    wishing

the escape

button could

    help me

    out.

Destiny Padilla

Colored Candy Turned White

Bodega on Crotona,
one dollar got me 10 candies
or a bag of chips, a colored soda
and five smaller candies.
My 7 year old hands tasted rich
every day, after school was out.

Chubby, gordita, eat eat!
You didn't eat all of your food!
Was a statement that meant,

You are in trouble.

Even though my stomach
was aching to perfection,
I knew Papi would get told that
I didn't eat all of my food.
Cousins giggled a giggle
that whispered, "you're in trouble, mala, malcriada".

Poverty that is urban.

Destiny Padilla

Not eating the food Abuela used her island recipes on
brewed disrespect.

Having food is a privilege not a right.

Eat all of your food
that way you'll become
big and strong.
Big and strong became
asthma and adhd.

Abuela is no longer here to see.

The bodega became a couch
with white walls and a therapist.
Not eating enough became
talking and thinking too fast.

I buy new candy now.

MELANIE MONROY

No Longer Burning

I grew up running through the pompas
in a community that is no longer burning

So

what is concerning?

The dictionary defines ghetto and its inhabitants
As an "isolated or segregated area or group"

But not me,
I run freely through the pompas in a community
that is no longer burning

I am bringing a first generation of life
back into my community

Oh

you're from there?
I am observed from a distance like a Ceiba tree

Trying to spread its roots

Melanie Monroy

from the underworld into the heavens

But they do not dare cut me down,

as I am watered by these pompas
running in the streets

Melanie Monroy

Sweet Ferry Terminal

Sweet Ferry Terminal
You are never lonely

Sunrise and sunset
Is the traveler's ceremony

Saturated with waiting,
tired eyes,

and youth running around
Experiencing their best highs

If I get on this ferry
Where will I go?

Will it be heavenly?
Gliding through the Upper Bay
On a charming summer day.

Or will it be angsty?
Finger numbing
In the winter peak.

JOEL L. DANIELS
to be honest, i wish i had an MFA, too

i am still confused by niggas who go to school to write poems

i mean i am not knocking niggas who go to school to

write poems

but it baffles me, knock kneed me who used to need food on

friday nights

would eat frozen sausage links and watch tgif on abc

not touching the dial

not looking at the sky not counting the change in the

piggy bank

not telling my mother i opened the toys on christmas

the night before

i just only peeked a little but mainly played with them

guffawing at the repetition of the mashing of buttons

what it sounds like to be freedom for a change

for a chance to beat your dick silly until it is too tired

to be only limp and of service to no one but you

and the little voices dancing about your head

and beady bright brown eyes

and to be frank i don't know what those schools smell like

how they got here,

which hands bided their time building them

guided bricks, the gilded rugrats of a nation

solemnly swearing to rip the whole truth from the womb

i may have been too busy practicing blackness

electric sliding my way into picnics

a byproduct of broad strokes and gary coleman one liners

not to say you cannot do both

i mean i have seen the coin go ivy league or ivy park right?

you can be beyonce and a backwoods roller

maybe that's backwards maybe beyonce and bach

and who wouldn't want the acclaim or the ease of

access acquired with a mfa?

motherfuckers be swinging degrees of celsius

swinging ding-a-ling, swigging ol' e

digging for gold no diaper changes when you wield a syllabus

each one teach one inside the institution

inside the snide remarks made by jittery white boys

who buy gin on their mother's credit

learned all the rules of the jitney dance

reciting soulja boy and dipping their sliced bread in aioli

pasting and copy catting,

pathing their ways with a bent pencil

they speak cantonese,

Joel L. Daniels

know the width of butter churn their own maybe?

and when they walk the halls their feet clutter and chant
and you hear rhythm nation in the background
everyone in sync humming
everyone doing jazz hands
everyone knowing their name
everyone dipping the crunchy parts of their tone in hummus

and the the the pretty ethnic girls furl fire and front as nanny's
for the beleaguered types ornery and so disturbed by the
latest news in russia and meanwhile we want all the
kim k nudes

did you hear meghan the stallion can rap but everyone wants
to ask about her body black woman bodies are not covered in
mystery any longer and we do too much blaming about that
too much naming about that too much

and so here we are all of us collecting things and banging our
hands against furnaces to find the heat and look at the grants
and scholarships and niggas don't do math

i mean look at Stuyvesant

but that's okay that's alright because someone has to pay for school someone has to read these plays someone has to buy these poems someone has to support the poet.

DANYSSE I. SERRANO
The Bronx is Burning (again)

The Bronx is burning
Again and again
inflamed for years

Summer time comes
with heat and gunshots
fired at the children

Police steer clear
focus on meters and dimes
while our children die

Engulfed in the flames

The Bronx is burning
Been happening for years
We all wear black
in this summer heat

We mourn and our protectors
stay squeaky clean

Danysse I. Serrano

But we stay burning
and yearning
for a chance

for our boys to thrive
for our boys to survive
to live to be men
instead of becoming pictures
posted on makeshift
memorials
on corners of their olds sets
while their boys cry
their moms shrivel inside

The Bronx is a war ground
"get home safe bro"
bc this summer heat
It comes like a wave

of fear
terror
death and despair
the Bronx is burning
Hey Cuomo, do you care?

Nirvana

I think I knew you in my last life
Maybe my brother or my son
Maybe the only being who knew
Me from the inside
The sound of my heart beat

I am a woman
Warm in my womb and
I think I've spent
a life with you

While I raise you now
The sound of my heart beat
Familiar to you.

The first day I met you
I knew you
I must have loved you
Taught you to love
In a past life and this one.

How many times will we meet?

Danysse I. Serrano

Did we reach perfection

Nirvana in our blood

Before ever knowing

In this life

We could soil this

Boil it down

To nothing now

From soil we grew

From my soul

you anew.

If only I knew

That's all we were

Souls meeting again.

This life we're in passing.

The last, everlasting.

Danysse I. Serrano

Tell the boys

Tell the boys these words
that as long as our hood
beats to the sound of hurt
We remain on two paths

One of healing
and one of hurting.

Tell the boys
that when they take their hurt
and carve it into the skin
of other people's babies
with knives and bullets
they continue the chain
link the dead to the living
to the dead living in this hell
the chain of hurt does not end
it binds us
trauma in inheritance
generational rage.

Tell the boys

Danysse I. Serrano

they can be healers too
they can heal too.

AMERESOUL
Where I was raised

I was raised in an era where being hungry meant you just had
to sleep it off
and gang violence, street violence led to the sounds of sirens
that weed far from silent;
I memorized that tune.
Coked out dope fiends were the most humble human beings
until that craving called and the need is in their blood
streams, you won't even recognize them in about four weeks.
And their mistakes now sit on your mind and you remember
the day they said don't do drugs young man as they helped us
with our bags up the staircase now they're laying in the
staircase with a needle in their vain;
eyes closed shut but they're wide awake.
I was raised in an era where this was reality,
the ones closest to your hands were the ones who didn't want
to reach for your reaching hands;
They lost their sanity. That was the least of our worries,
we walked out the war in our building to the war in the
streets, strapped with our book bags and uniforms trusting
my older me. Living the same reality with different dreams.

Ran into the bloodbath of a man who got shot in the head
running away from a man he couldn't stand,
the beef was so real. Our life was surreal can't you see.
I was raised in an era where the latest trend was staying alive
long enough to walk with a purpose not the same purpose
others had, different purposes like breathing and
concentrating on keeping your eyes open, while a stranger
with a name tag and 3 letters you would never forget
EMT
Emotionally,
Mentally,
Traumatizing
holds your hands as they keep your mother away,
she screams in the corner in agony and pain, they say a
mother should never bury her child but he was already six
feet deep when the cruelties of our society led him to the
streets; this is the war that we live in. We had no choice,
we had to survive a war amongst each other
and the sweetest sound was a sigh of relief,
because I made it home,
I can breathe,
but I am still hungry.

KIMBERLY ROSA

F

L

Y

I am slipping in between hands of water;

falling down a path of curiosity

I am holding onto the heights where one feels the top of

the winds hat across the earth fiercely

holding my arms up in the air trying to feel the clouds

I can see with eyes of wonder

—a light that beams to blind a soul

So maybe it is God

his smile that shows me that I'm almost there.

LEE ORTIZ
Tradition

Hmmmmm

Do you smell that?,

The heavy scent of sofrito sizzling in corn oil

I love this time of year, It's the only time of year

I see primas and primos I've never met

Newborn babies calling me tia ... Child

I don't even know who your mother is

Bochinche over cocquito

While everyone gangs on my mother

for always being late with the pernil.

We share laughters and old stories

I enjoy seeing my grandmother

share her warrior tales

Reminds me of who I came from

I sit in a room full of women

who's battle scars

run deeper than los mares

Single mothers who made

traditions like these possible

with vente pesos to their name

I sit and I admire them

as they serve me a plate of food
fit for a queen and tell me
"come te lo todo mi hija"

Lee Ortiz

Ode to The Bronx

I was bred from turnstiles and concrete.

These streets were mom and dad to me.

Car horns and tire screech are symphonies to my heartbeat.

BX is what I breath and baby look at what you made me,

A QUEEN!

STELLE REZ
Dear Emotions

Dear Emotions,

This letter has been long overdue. You're doing your job a little too well. Unfortunately, you have overburdened your coworkers with tasks and have caused them to work overnight and graveyard shifts.

The eyes and tear ducts have been depressed and driven to become damaged and dry, no longer can they cry, no matter how hard they try.

The brain has been mauled with memories and making mysteries that it can't solve, soon enough, he may be gone.

The heart is excessively beating to the point of bleeding and if this continues, she will be leaving.

Please stop trying to pitch us to another person that is not interested in making an investment in us. This is damaging the system and it'll make us feel as if we will never get a good investment, and we'll settle for one who will damage us from the inside out.

You need to work with everyone else in sync, or we will sink

Sincerely,

A concerned soul

WILL CRUZ
Gems

I've donated my time and effort to the cause
And I refuse to redo or relive those mistakes
I'm unsure if I'm an idiot or flawed
Yet I ignore the call, cause your smile is all it takes
I don't feel used, or abused or insert the adjective here
I feel smitten and excited as I ignore fear
Because Gems deserve security
We both know this and sure, I'm focused (but)
Whether the reflection is diamond or coal
I need you to know (that)
Gems deserve security
In the rough or on display
Hidden in plain sight or exposed every day
It's not the imperfections nor its appearance
Whether it's full retail or it's clearance
I need you to know (that)
Gems deserve security

PETER ROSADO

I, Latino

What are you?

Three simple words uttered out of a face

that seemed to mean no harm

How did they know the battle waged within..

The battle to defend who I was in the face of those that

doubted

Human I reply, just like you

This is where the laugh falls like drops of acidity

Like what ARE you?

You know…..where you from?

You look Italian

A strained smile crosses my face as I repeat my already

chambered response..

A response I've repeated countless times in my own head

Trying to convince myself of its honesty

I'm Puerto Rican

Really???

You don't look Puerto Rican……

The words hang there like icicles in winter

Peter Rosado

While my entire being screams internally
WHAT DO YOU MEAN I DON'T "LOOK"
PUERTO RICAN
WHAT AM I SUPPOSED TO LOOK LIKE!!!
But all they hear is a laugh when I say, I get that all the time

But later at night,
I tell myself over and over
I AM Puerto Rican..I AM Puerto Rican
Until I get pulled into that world..
A world that smells like mi abuela's kitchen
and the song of the coqui always hangs in the air..
Where Tito, Hector, and Celia are still alive and singing
and where Tia doesn't miss the number by just one

I AM Puerto Rican..
Holding a belief of magic so tight that
botanicas can cure anything
Belief in revolution so high that nobody can hold a candle to
the Young Lords
You don't give us independence we TAKE IT because it
belongs to us..
Pero before we leave the house everyday we give thanks..
En el nombre del Padre, el hijo, e el spirtu santo..AMEN…

Peter Rosado

I AM Puerto Rican...
Where the music always makes our legs move..especially
abuelo at the wedding
We talk loud, cook loud, sing loud..
Maybe you don't understand we are just LOUD!

We are not racially pure
Culturally, we possess ritmos y sueños que no se
pueden sacar de our essences
They are reflected in our speech and our manner
No matter what language or banner we choose
It all frees us from being aqui o alla, here, there, everywhere
This MIXED RACE IS THE PLACE...

And every day after..
I want to find that person who asked me what I was..
Grab them by the arms and tell them with the revolution
drums aiding my voice...
YES..I am Puerto Rican..
The blood of the Tiano runs through my vein
I am a PURE BORIQUA
raised from the island of Borinquen, my paises given name..

I AM THE BRAVE ONE..

But before all of that..

I LATINO..

It's in the blood and sure we are crazy

but we are proud

and will always be

So don't tell me..

I don't LOOK Puerto Rican..

Cuz I've been living it day-to-day since before 1492.

SOFIE VASQUEZ

// feeling like i (finally) get myself

we repeat cycles because it's familiar

sometimes growth can be slow,

but it will always be prominent

if we allow it to be

nineteen began with pain and revelation

it was the push,

the change

the transformation

that overwhelmed me

but i allowed it to wash over me

the transfiguration came through the appearance of

music,

photography,

and a new friend

Sofie Vasquez

all in the same day

the realization broke me down
sinking me almost to my knees,
as choked sobs and red eyes consumed my body
in a public space for everyone to witness

it occurred me to then
only nineteen days
after my nineteenth birthday
that until that moment
I have always felt alone
displaced, misunderstood,
mistreated, threatened,
forgotten, misdirected

but no longer.

the change immediately took charge

it's been five months since my transformation,
when you say it out loud it seems like nothing at all

Sofie Vasquez

but this is the happiest I've ever been

there was time, my art became a burden
it weighed and choked me down,
killing my passion
leaving me like zombie

now I relish and flower

Sofie Vasquez

Mechita

grandma, you are the highest mountain of the Andes

a misty tower that kisses the sky, the heavens beam on you

your skeleton bore the backbone for your family

brown, worn hands molded a future from scratch,

turned the pieces of wavering hope and stagnant faith

that danced in your mind to an opportunity that you couldn't
even taste

but your daughters and sons did

grandma, you are the root that bore this big, great tree

born where the sand kissed the sea, you were as defiant as the
tidal waves

but you were expected to conform and submit,

forced to dim your blinding glow

that could outshine a thousand suns

but your rebellion seeped through the motions and actions of
your love

a sharp tongue, your lips spilled passages of wit,

soft, reminders of your endless devotion

the declarations of your unwavering faith, and the

gentle lullabies that spanned two generations,

in a fluid mix of Spanish and English

between the sips of your favorite red wine

dress me up in your favorite earrings, grandma

you adorn my face, a mirror where you can see your
daughter's eyes,

in rings, necklaces and bangles of precious gold

you see this jewelry as a testament to your survival

a small reward for the sacrifices you've made

you try not to tell me so much about the past,

you were always a woman of the future

you choose to relish in the now, but I can't help but look back,

because I can't stop admiring and thanking you for what you had done,

from the late nights you were stuck in Manhattan, scrubbing floors and cleaning desks

as your children called for you back in The Bronx, from the nights he raised his voice and told you

to know your place, from the nights where your faith and strength were questioned.

you prevailed

your power will forever amaze me, and you are not shy to remind me my worth

you will not hesitate to uplift me, and tell me what wonders I am capable of,

Sofie Vasquez

and as you brush my hair back, placing a loose stray behind
my ear

you never fail to remind me what a beautiful woman I am as

you place two golden earrings in my ears, almost as a way of
saying

I'll always be here

MARGARITË (MAGI) CAMAJ

We Always Had Everything We Needed

They say that we come from nothing,

but they forgot to look inside of us.

Can't you see our hearts?

Can't you see how much love we have inside of us?

Or, are you only capable of seeing the surface?

Love is everything.

It can conquer anything.

Because of the love that lives inside of us,

we hold the most power.

So, how could we come from nothing

when we have everything inside of us?

We come from everything.

They just can't notice it.

They are too busy looking at

what their eyes can see,

instead of looking deeper.

Dear New York City,

I fall more in love with you every single day—just the way that you are. And, I know that they keep trying to change you. They keep trying to gentrify you. I'm sorry for that. My heart bleeds when they try to destroy you, change you, and turn you into something that you aren't. They're not letting you be yourself. They keep trying to shape you into something that they will love. I'm sorry that they don't love you in the way that I do, to your very core. I hope that you keep your soul just the way it is, no matter how much they try to drown you out. I pray that you never change, internally, even though they are trying to change all that you are on the outside.

Margaritë Camaj

Through The Darkness

Love guided her through

the darkness when no other

kind of light was strong enough to allow

her eyes to see the way.

Because of love, no darkness felt

as heavy.

DANNALIS PARRA

2/6/18

They call it a mental disorder

It makes me feel like I can't get my shit in order

Or that my mind is in pieces like a puzzle that is not in order

A few pieces are missing to make things makes sense

Is that why it doesn't make any sense?

When I sit there and stare at the wall?

My mind wanders to places that I didn't even realize I've been

to

Places that make me think about thoughts that I don't have

control over

My mind wanders a mile a minute while my body just sits

there...tense

And it's not 'til I hear something that makes me snap out of

the trance that I've been sitting in

...not even realizing I'm just sitting there

Not realizing how much time I've given to doing nothing

Not realizing how much thought I've put into the thoughts

that are running through my mind and my body can't catch

up

I look at the time and think, "damn, what the hell was I doing

all of this time just sitting there?"

My body just there...I look at the time and see the minutes

ticking away and I just stare

Why can't I move?

Why can't I go?

Why can't I just get up and say, "hey you're going to be okay"?

Why can't I just do what I have to do, in the time that I have,

instead of letting that time tick away?

My body is choosing to stay

While my brain continues to drift away

Be it as it may

I guess that's why they call it a mental disorder

Because I highly doubt anyone chooses to let time slip away

from them

While their mind is struggling to put the pieces to the puzzle

back together

...in order for it to make sense

And then wonder if the pieces were ever together to begin

with

The pieces to the puzzle that is your mind

Your mind

Your mentality

Your mental space

The space that you go to when you drift into space

Maybe that's why they call it a mental disorder

Because your mental is in disorder and the pieces to the

puzzle are all over the place

All over the space that is your mind

Bueno…you better get your shit in order

So you don't have to call it a mental disorder

But…maybe, like Kanye said…that's your super power

MIKE MCMANUS

Untitled

My boots ate

every gum stained

reach of pavement,

shirt snagged

on every hole

bit through chain links,

my fingertips seen

every leaf of grass,

needle, herb,

vegetable, hedge,

weed, and flower

put in dirt here.

my eyes shattered

every shard of glass,

Mike McManus

lips tasted every

cigarette butt,

touched every

fallen feather,

arms welcomed

every ant

and rat here.

my head shook

every summer soda

spray can,

my skin caressed every wick

before it

was lit here.

coddled every sob

boxed and barred

from being told here.

born here.

gotten old here.

Mike McManus

I hear the invisible

only God knows,

the spirit here.

I manned the flights, walk ups,

stories, scaffolds, escapes,

bridge grates and views here.

I mixed rusto chrome

with blues here.

born on a Tuesday

told on Friday

I would lose

here.

Im still here.

I move here.

my heart heard

all the hurt

burnt

backfired

plans

smothered with sand here.

I stand here.

laid out blankets

on tar

sung aloud to every cloud

& smart kite

that never caught the itis

& still feel them

fly here.

RIGHT here.

showed every joe shmo

where its at here.

musta rapped to every foot stomp

& clap here.

hopped every cab

every loosie spot copped here.

cuffed by every cop here.

beat the skin off my teeth

with every banana leaf

& eeked out

every pinch of grit here.

I don't sit here.

I fixed alone

from every moan here.

laid hands on every bone shown

through skin here.

I been here.

I'll be here.

I AM here.

Untitled

I remember in the classroom

Scents of spring setting in

sweat seeping

Hair frizzing

newly charged testicles titillated,

Feet feining to bust out of these Buster Browns and chow
down on chain links and GT peddles,

ripe asphalt that wipes off

swiping wiffle ball bats and sliding into a johnny pump third,

I heard the good humor clanging when that first whip of
pollen

Wafted through the window

And how soon the crew cuts cropped our tops.

Hot trips to Long Beach,

buddies in the Country Squire

importing salt & sand

Mike McManus

Back to The Bronx.

In a minute

We scurry up the block

and see if the girls

are as hot as us,

a rouse through

giggles & a goofy smile

"walk me to the store",

charring pilfered cigarettes,

Nods and nervous twitches,

Innocence drifting off

Into school yards

Handball courts and catching tags,

before beepers

We sat on mailboxes

On the block waiting,

Cassette player boom box praying,

for familiar faces to turn the corner.

Mike McManus

Horn blasts,

the older kids

Cruising past,

in there mothers' cars,

My confidence like cheese sliding from a scalding slice

eyeing a crush

lip dripping like

italian icys,

shivers and

stupid lines

teaching me about next times,

and the Whole Wide World

Was the neighborhood back then,

There's

So much more

I wanna tell myself

back then

ZOE CRUZ
Happy Hour

We're sitting at the bar
and you tripped on her name
three times.
You call this your bad habit.
The smell of your festering wound
makes my nose burn.

So I spit my whiskey into your mouth
when you lean in for a kiss.
You didn't like this. I say
"It's to stop the infection from spreading"

Anxiety, Depression, & Me: A Threesome

"I'm leaving you both at home tonight"
"You're the reason I couldn't eat with my family on
thanksgiving"
"No you can not come with me on this date"
"I can't bring you to work"
"We shouldn't reply to this message"
"I just thought I'd go out for a little bit"
"I shouldn't wear this, what do you like?"
"You sure? I actually think they like me"
"You're wrong this time"
"You were right. You're always right"
"One at a time! I can't hear when you both speak"
"Not here, please not here"
"Leave me alone"
"I'm sorry, don't leave me alone"
"I can't function without you two"
"I'm afraid of the silence"
"Does the bed of their chest have space for all of us"
"They don't have enough room"
"It's just us again"
"Can you hear me like I hear you?"

Zoe Cruz

Subtle Waves

The tug of my sweater on a moving
train.. pulling me closer into the
safety that existed between
your two fingers and my pocket.

The laughter that swirled around
our heads making us dizzy enough
to rest on each other's shoulder

The touch of my nose followed
by a crinkled smile
Your eyes wandered off
unable to hold my gaze
you looked up..
what did you say to sky?

Did you say it wasn't fair
that if we met each other
on this bridge it would burn
that it would be impossible
to share anything together for
too long.

Zoe Cruz

Did you say that it could
have been so simple?

MICHELLE ADORNO

Bullets

Words hold weight. Words hold meaning.

We flung them carelessly like stray bullets into the night and waited for them to ricochet back to our broken bodies.

We explode into fits of rage and indignation, questioning motives from the darkest corners or our souls and somewhere between our heads and our hearts lies the empty, emotionless, void that used to be filled with the love that we had for one another.

The silence is deafening…

Growing louder and louder inside of us. Swirling faster and faster. It moves, it creates, it destroys and so I destroy you. I destroy you with the things you love most. Twisting and pulling until they are unrecognizable…until you are unrecognizable. Until I don't see your edges or the curve or your lips, only 2 dimensional blocks of a dull reddish color that I once kissed. I don't see you. Only impressions of you. Vague vestiges of who you once were and I am a vague vestige of who I once was. A pseudo-intellectual Picasso version of the person you once knew and loved, but can no longer stand to be around. My "I love you's" sound like nails against a chalk board, feel like having your insides torn out, tastes like vinegar that you spit back out in the form of threats and condemnation. Letters form syllables. Syllables form words, words, words, but never the right ones. Never the real ones, because honesty is something we exchanged in favor of seeming unbreakable. But perhaps we are more broken than ever, like cracked bottles that have been strewn across the shore line.

But maybe one day we will be sea glass. We will shine brightly as the sun reflects off of the water and we'll marvel at how broken doesn't mean forever.

But in this moment. We are lost...

Lost in memories...

Lost in Time....

Lost in words...

Words hold weight. Words hold meaning. We flung them carelessly like stray bullets into the night.

TONEYSHA MICHAUX

GUAVA: Distant Love

I saw you today

Your face was clear as day

At first I saw my father

In red and black

Strong and almighty

And the more I watched him

His features began to change slightly

Until there was no more of him

And Only you

I wanted to reach out

Tell the world I could see you

But you said no

Only you

Toneysha Michaux

You played the piano for me in all white

And told me stories about your lost love

That seemed to last forever

Sometimes I wish I met you at that bridge

So we could jump together

Or maybe even listen to you one last time

Be that shoulder that went missing

Be the gravity to hold you down

To keep your feet from lifting

Each time you said you were tired

I really wish we had listened

To the sorrow behind every alphabet

In that sentence

To the sweet violin sound

With its strings missing

Toneysha Michaux

But it is you and only you

Soulful love from a tiny distance

You are missed

GUAVA: Stargazem

It was you

Me

Her

She

It was us

And them

Then we

Laughed inside and out

Until our tears fell out

Joy

It was the beach

The navy of the navy'est

The brightest

It was almost as if

The sky threw up stars

Til there was no more room

Toneysha Michaux

Space

Stay with me

No really stay with me

Toneysha Michaux

WILDFLOWER: Untitled

I watched everyone

I watched as they looked

Helpless, worn out, and bothered

I saw you, you looked just like them

My eyes wandered off again

To the different cloths but each one

Giving me the same shade

Not even bothered to look my way

I felt it was normal that way

But then I saw you again

The smile on your face

I imagined you went back to a memory

A memory where you saw love

And felt it at the same time

A memory where you saw your first born

Toneysha Michaux

Open its eyes for the first time

But then your smile faded

So fast in slow motion as if you were waiting

for the sudden pain to soak in

I then too felt sad

I felt your energy without a simple

Eye contact and I felt for you

A complete stranger

Your soul must be beautiful

WILDFLOWER: Untitled

Who taught you to run wild with broken hearts

embedded in your skin as animal print

Who told you love wasn't a noun

Who taught you that it was okay to use sex for

your own guilt

taking away freedom that didn't belong to you

Who taught you to build a home without a

foundation

Who told you to peel back the fabric

from your bare arms because the heart

on your sleeve was making

you weak

Who taught you these things

they can't be human

Toneysha Michaux

WILDFLOWER: Untitled

We happened

And I can't fix this cracked wall between us

You like me but you refuse

To make me feel comfortable to believe so

Why

Maybe because I didn't treat you

The way you're use to

The way girls fumble all over you

Drop their tasteful morals

From between their legs

In a heartbeat if you asked them to

I believe this and still

I can never refuse your kiss

My heart tightens

It's like the hunger games

Toneysha Michaux

Swimming inside me

When I see you

Do anything you ask of me

I volunteer as tribute

T.J. MCGOWAN

Full Stomach

I want to talk about all things vibrant

swallowed in violence,

and silent screams

beaming in place of light

through the dimmed

and desolate dead ends

brimming over

with echoes

of where the heart used to be.

I want to talk about image

and imagining

I'm nothing,

confronting the formula

T.J. McGowan

I used to walk

way back when,

when the dark stalked me,

can't be a human being

because I'm still asking myself

whose this human been?

And the mirror is a fucking plague,

couldn't be clearer – this rage …

You're a monster,

fattened flesh without purpose,

purposeful sabotage

from eyes to mind

and back again.

Every glass surface,

a knee-jerk reaction,

no satisfaction found

in the boundaries

T.J. McGowan

of the past's rehearsals

convincing myself

I'm worthless.

I want to talk about porcelain nights

and the frightened finger

lingering over the push-button

in my throat,

afloat in bile,

denial is key

to purge full stomach,

knowing damn well

the food wasn't the issue,

but what I wanted to vomit up

was me ...

T.J. McGowan

Cellular

In this distance of shortened light

I found specks

of a Mother's song

on my pulse,

pulling the stagnant blood

back into the places gone dead

from neglect

and numbing of inner warfare.

The salt is old

in my eyes

and waiting for water

to give it life again,

a kaleidoscope veil

victimizing my vision – a candied horror,

this vanished well,

T.J. McGowan

a chord cut

between truth and feeling,

the melody of hope

strumming under fingertips

of windswept love

once forgotten,

pushes rivers

through my veins – a cleansing,

trash and gut-rot

and the dust of rusted bone

free-falls from the revitalized homes

regaining foundations

in the places I cannot touch.

From time's hand

to my heart,

sadness seems

to tally mark

more than seconds can

in a minute,

and suffering

is the only understanding

to breath – the only way

to value being alive,

and, so, I keep kissing the sounds

of design left basking in my ears

from the broken dreams

and pitch-black nights,

because pain is cellular

and cosmic.

Without it,

we are nothing.

JESSICA DIAZ

Roots

The smell of café con leche takes me back to my childhood

Reminds me of Mami getting up, ready to start the new day –

Crisp & rich, just like the coffee she stirred…

Just like her voice…

"Ya es hora de levantarse, Mija"

The taste of arroz con dulce makes me smile

Time travels me to simple days when worries of Who liked
Who better could be gently eased away

with a spoonful of crèma, canela & raisins –

Reminders that sweetness lingers & resonates from the Inside
Out

"Te he dicho, Hija - Sola la hago, Y Sola la Pago", Mami'd say
time & time again…

Do it for Ourselves, Earn it for Ourselves

Tenemos que hacer nuestra realidad –

Nunca dejes que alguien te diga lo que puedes o no puedes
hacer

Somos El Arco Iris entre las nubes

Break away to the shouts of "Azucarrrrrrrrr!!!" resonating en
la cocina

No short supply of sweetener here!

Just the cries of Friday night fiestas in Tia's house

Adonde toda la familia got their salsa on cada fin de semana

Channeling their inner Celia & Tito, con "un chin" del
Canario

No birthday, No problema

Vamos a celebrar "Salud, Dinero Y Amorrrrrrrrrrrr!!!"

Ridin' down the rumblin' tracks of the 4 & the 6

The epic voyage into El Barrio to visit mis abuelos -

Jessica Diaz

Where the epic love story of mis padres began

Refusing to sit, instead choosing to kneel on the train seat

I peered out its' window, with the occasional head nod and
shoulder pops

To the booming system,

With Young Pro Ski Wild-Style bumping LL on his radio

Mami, letting Me Be, pero nunca quitandome el ojo de
encima -

I watched the tatted subway cars that zoomed past the
opposite side

Tryna read the bubble letter tags, decipher the lines, glean the
messages

Unlock the hierarchical codes -

Catching glimpses of urban castles that littered the landscape

Catching glimpses of Myself reflected in the flecks of
sunshine that danced on those hazy windows

El aroma de aciente y ajo penetrated your nostrils as soon as
you came up to 116th

We could never just walk past the cuchifrito spot without
buying

some alcapurrias y rellenos de papa

Fried to golden perfection, sitting in its' lightbulb spotlight in
the window

For the hungry passerby to be mesmerized by the potential of
its' saborrrrrrrrrrr…

Welcoming the taste of the sizzle & sting

Todavia lo puedo escuchar…

The crackling of flames on glowing candlewicks

Burning beneath the altar of Abuela's santos in her bedroom

I imagined myself within the glow –

An ember levitating towards the heavens,

Free of restraint -

Gaining strength and Brilliance the higher I float

Jessica Diaz

Caressed and cradled by The Father's calloused Hands,

Doves ruffled in advance to be prepared in the likelihood that
We were made to fall

We still rejoiced in the turbulent flight

Seeing the char in our bones

Singed brows, Sweat-stained & Tear-soaked wings -

Yet, ever ready to attempt achieving new heights once more

And so… I grew up.

Learning how & when to place my offering,

Allowing los espiritos to light my way -

Because, now, within these reveries is that I realize

From within the crackle is

Where this Puerto-Rican girl was made

Jessica Diaz

White-Washed: Graffiti's Exclusive Interview

I'm not invisible

Call me Ms. Invincible.

My movements been rooted in the dome like the instinctual

Fueling this fire we seek since Being was in utero

"A different Animal, but the same Beast"

Like Yeezy inviting all daring spectators to come take a peek

Don't dare call me by your government's names

"Urban Decay"

"Topographic Terrorism"

"Utter Vandalism"

"Straight Trash"

Address me accordingly!

You know you see this majestic mane

"Your Highness… They await you…"

Jessica Diaz

When "The Ruler" speaks,

wait your turn and listen for the breakthrough

Hear me speak; but can you bear to hear

Not quite the open metaphorical book

But, put in that werk

Reach high upon these shelves

Clutch my spine

Turn my pages

Sift through my many incarnations

Read me. Feel me.

No classical labels

No big institution stables

Just beaming colors & curves

Slick wit tha werd, and a passion to be heard

No Pause. Only Push Play, and Repeat.

Jessica Diaz

I be Old Skool roots with New World perspectives

I gets OPEN,

Yet, equally cautious - keeping Our dynamic histories close.

Fearing trusting allowances to bask in our Earthly richness

will prompt Him to appropriate

What is inherently Ours once more

My worth does not lie in your hands, as you've made it seem

THIS Beauty is Epic – lining the urban cityscapes

Reverberations of peoples voices speaking my name

I spread the Vibe…

Vibrations

Mos Defiantly.

Playing our hood symphonies in audio-less

Vertical / Horizontal manifestations

Not knowing all the answers of what to do

Jessica Diaz

But, it's cool –

It's the questions that guide us anyways

My magic lies in this mosaic'd mess

Self-Identification, proclaiming as:

Ms. Multi-Cultural

Ms. Multi-Faceted

Ms. Multi-Disciplinary

Yet, STILL branded as:

Miss Understood

Miss Represented

Miss Communicated

But, like I said – It's cool…

Not waiting on Him to deem me priceless

Our inner value is limitless.

Jessica Diaz

Motivations and Movements, Pure of Heart

As we hold true to remain this bold spectrum of Outlaw Art

LORENDA MABLE

I'm Learning

I'm learning that what I thought I wanted ain't as important
no more,

and the doors that I opened, ain't too hard at closing no more,

I learned that, what I've done can no longer be held against
me no more,

and the bigger things, that I thought were important before,

can no longer hold me captive with its allure,

don't get me wrong, I still stumble and can be shallow,

True to Taurus fashion, I'm stubborn and my words can be
hard to follow,

but the shedding of this shell, this self inflicted hell, this
unintended spell is no longer notorious,

while this budding of self love is rather victorious,

I'm learning.

DAVE MABLE

A brother's love

Special shout out to my sista Lorenda "Lada" Mable. I appreciate you giving me the opportunity to express myself, share my opinion, advice and learning experience while incarcerated. Though these last years have been a challenge and I've come across a lot of adversity, what makes it so much worth is I've grown as a person. I was once told that "the best teacher in life is experience". I truly believe that...

With help and support from my close family, I've fought through some long years, not to mention, believing in my spiritual guidance, having faith also gave me the strength to continue my fight. The journey taught me so much about myself and others, how to love, how to communicate, how to cope with different struggles, acceptance, learning how to give and receive second chances, forgiveness, seeing others point of view and just so much more that I could go on with. But most of all, the importance of this is to, hopefully bring awareness to the young generation and show others that through aladalove (a lot of love), things can be changed, in people, relationships and everyday life.

One of the first struggles I've had to endure was being sentenced to 20- 40 years in a state correctional facility (jail) and accepting it at the age of 18. Owning up to my mistakes and accepting my punishment was one of the hardest things I've had to do but it put me at ease and allowed me to get closer to God. He had so much love and forgiveness in his heart, it was amazing... I don't want to force my beliefs on anyone but I would like to reflect on a verse and its meaning from the bible that I was recently reading before I leave this topic. In Hebrews 8:12, he said, " I will forgive their sins and will no longer remember their wrongs." But I bring that up to say, forget about those mistakes, and failures in the past, that's what God has done. And if he doesn't remember them anymore, why should you? Open your heart up and love just as much as he did. Before I go on, please don't for one second think that I am this super spiritual person and I walk a straight path cause ill be the first to tell you that I still have my faults. I'm a regular human being just like you, I just decided not to let my mistakes define who I really am.

Being as though I came to prison at a young age, it helped me mature into the person I am today. Not knowing what my future held, opened my eyes to the present and allowed me to see the best in every situation. After the lies, betrayal, hopes, worries and hurt, I still sort out to see the best in people. Love also played a major part in my life because its a powerful feeling. It can feel good, and hurt at the same time. Being on both ends of it taught me patience.

At the age of 20, about the time I received my sentence, I suddenly became numb to love. My absence from friends, family members, even relationships I had with females became non existent. (its true, out of sight, out of mind). It wasn't until a few years ago when I begin to rebuild my relationship with my lil sister Lada is when I started to feel loved again. Being in this type of environment, you start to become accustomed to the negative people and believe that nobody loves you and you're in this alone. My sista showed me so much love, gave me amazing advice, confidence and never judged me. That same love helped me cope with all of the adversity I was getting beat with. The denial of the courts and my appeal, to no longer having a support team, to just hopelessness. And through the mist of it all, Lada taught me how to use my voice and words to show my love because its not just physical, love is in so many different forms.

So now I ask that you use my situation as a testament to prove that under any circumstance, you can find love, show love and beloved, all at the same time. And always remember, "its better to have loved than to never love at all"...

TAISHA GUY

Love is/ Love was

Love is life in prison

Love was life in prison

Love was county

Rikers

State facility

upstate

Love was suspected

Investigated

Under arrest

Love was conviction

Would the defendant please stand

Love was "life"

A sentence

Love was barely a bed

Taisha Guy

A fucking cot

Dirty ass gray walls

A sink above a bowl

Brushing teeth

Where a ass had been

Love was life in prison

Love was hope

When mail came around

Love was

"ah man just hit up my commissary"

Love was praise be to allah

Thank you Jesus

If I just make it out this bitch

I ain't coming back again

Love was life in Prison

Love was long nights

Making adjustments

Taisha Guy

Love was just don't be misunderstood

Because there ain't nothing like

A misunderstanding

Love was picking a side

Always picking a side

Love was not trying to be nobody's bitch

Love was hectic

In a I didn't know Love would be like this

... way

Hard

Love was life in prison

Love was a fork in the road

Love was realizing greatness

Love was seeing a person

who looked like me but not hating him

Love was me taking a damn,

how I mess up like this?

and using that for education

Educating the masses

Turning oppression into positives

Love was making it

When making it just meant a step forward

Love was letting go of life in prison

Love became something different

Being me, in my skin

But different

Change

Being the change

Like butterflies on the other

side of the world making

waves from ripples

Love is Terrence

Love is Thomas

Love is Alonzo

Love is Hernan

Taisha Guy

Love is Flow

Love is

Love was

Love is no longer a prison

Love is waking up everyday to fulfillment

BRENNAN ORTIZ

Responses of The Me-Kind

My mood is predetermined, excuse the weather who decides

Though if you'd look closely,

You'll see something new grows behind these eyes

And it's been there all along

Sometimes brown, sometimes iridescent

It seems you forget that we can be anyone

And within a lifespan, we are everyone

But still you come to me with your premonitions

And I can hardly do more than gasp

Wide-eyed, gasping

Gasping with wild eyes

Brennan Ortiz

And if I flee, I run the risk

Of running into places

Places that keep playing memories I can't keep,

though I'm done expelling

And when exposed, something's different

Conditioned,

Because there's all this magic, but I can't ever help myself

It's so much to contemplate what it means to heal

To evolve into a conduit

To heal or evolve

To find a north star

Or any shining beacon in darkness

Or any shade in blinding or burning light

And always I'll look for the brown in your eyes

Because they're gentler then the unending depths of the
middle

Though with any evasion

the words still hit me

Even when I don't hear them uttered

Shit is complicated

How to feel when everything in the moment is an

infinite variable

How to feel when shit's so complicated

Brennan Ortiz

October's Veil

It was October

and we chose to hide

hiding,

from the world, and from each other

together, and alone

and we didn't know it then

but we'd all hold on to each other

as though we found

it was all we had left

that was October

wonder why hide

and choose good reason,

among many

there is pain, infliction,

Brennan Ortiz

floating, like pollen in the air, looking to cling

and then some of us

we long,

for the dream of being left alone

alone though not without connection

so we take to places of obstruction

and in October, they're the woods

blanketed by leaves

in October, a different kind of fire

holding on to each other in hiding,

we become the fire in October

KATELYN B. PRIETO

Borinquen in The Bronx

"Ni de aqui, ni de alla"

A call to both homes

From the in-between

Where do you come from?

Who are you?

You must be from one

Not the other

But we have learned that this is not the case

We come from an identity

Formed in the melting pot

From streets adorned

With curly heads speaking Spanglish

A new tongue

Katelyn B. Prieto

An invalidated vernacular

That shows exactly what we are

As Tato says:

"We gave birth to a new generation

AmeRícan"

Capital R, accent on the I

That tells you who I am

A Boricua from the Bronx

Moved by both the salsa and hip-hop

blaring from moving cars

From roots that stretch farther than I could ever know

That knows the hum of the pigeon

And the call of the coqui

And to tell you

That I'm an American

Katelyn B. Prieto

And I'm a Rican

A melting pot myself

Katelyn B. Prieto

Reaching

My heart aches for something I can never see

Someone I may never be granted the privilege to meet

My soul yearns for what lies far beyond my flesh

For the untouched

Metaphysical life

Beyond my understanding

So I kneel before the being

That I do not know

With the booming voice

That I have never heard

And I reach for hands

That I have never touched

Searching

Searching

Begging to be seen

Katelyn B. Prieto

Do you see me?

Can you hear me?

Are you looking down on me the way everyone says you are?

Can you see my outstretched palms?

The way my hands tremble before you

Even though I'm not even sure you're there

But I look

To what you must have given me

Surrounded by gifts

And when I look to the people you have dropped here with
me

I can reach out my hands

And listen closely
And watch

And see just the faintest glimmer

Of you

BIANCA GUZMAN

GENTRIFICATION

Just because you buy an overpriced champion hoody you're
not an urban outfitter

you're an urban outsider

you stand out like a fucking highlighter

Get the fuck off my block

You're raising my rent prices

you're raising the price of my dollar hood slices

you're taking my slang

Appropriating my culture

Wearing the death of my ancestors

On your breath like vultures.

I want my old hood back

Ms. Alberta out her window singing church hymns

We Rolling Phillies on the stoop

That's a fat boy slim

Bianca Guzman

Smoke in the air heavy

My summer tasted like coco, mango, cherry

My tan skin smells like cocoa butter

My edges laid and gold hoops shine

Like no other

So you

Can never know what you never lived

And you

Can never really take what you never did

And I can never give up my borough without a plight

we ARE the Bronx bombers, not giving up without a fight.

MARLEY

The Wakeup

Stood quiet for years

Today, I let go

I'm now flooded with tears

Maybe it's just my fears finally released

10 years down

I only unleashed a beast

Running down the street

He beat the beauty I used to see

Knew I was depressed

So he wanted to make sure I was as low as I can be

Whole situation adjourned

How is it you're freer than me?

Held hostage,

Assaulted,

Plus, you put a pill in my drink

Traumatized since then

I hardly can think

Marley

Scared to close my eyes
What if I go unconscious while I dream?

Marley

P.T.S

Anxiety out the norm

My feelings want to drop lower than hell's floor

Thoughts on my death want to outpour

Counting down life until the reaper says no more

Why do I get so close then get taken away?

What's the message I'm to get today?

Is my killer around the corner?

Should I treat myself to a glass of ammonia?

How many pills until I'm a goner?

Already a loner

But sticking around for the kids

Just scared they'll just grow up

Forget

Then skid

Questioning life alone,

Like is this what it is?

If love carries through lifetimes,

Then is this the last time I live?

REGINA G. SHEPHERD
So Dream Darling Dreams, Darling

What can I tell you about following your dreams?

There have been many before you
Who have packed their hopes
away in cabinets.

Who stowed their inspiration
behind closed closet doors.

There came at a time, as may now,
deflectors of dreams
and mercenaries of hope.

I've heard God Almighty
listening well the intricacies
of intention
possibly while turning a differently
shaped vessel at the Potter's wheel.

Ambitions, some, have even survived rainstorms.
Still.

Regina G. Shepherd

Bout most I can tell you is that:

The dreams do come
and though truth may bend at times
to wipe them away,

There are people who have died
so that you can still
dream.

So Dream, Darling.
                Dream.

Regina G. Shepherd

Sunset

I am the sound of a maturing sunset,

                  brazen

and caught on yesterday's gray sweater.

The motion of sun that swaps its burn

      for the nighttime wind.

An ambition of Milky Way on a 'Parkside'   horizon

line   am I.

Feverish with the care of an unpromised tomorrow.

      Faith happens

                      from my jawline

when I dare call the day

      mine,

      the color of my breath melting into a misty

      morning.

This is how I fit:

      slipped into an evening

here on a Bronx MTA bus line   or
a flat
Tanzanian plain.

A tree is a tree   is a   miracle
viewed from far away.

And maybe orange and blue is not
                                        the color

outside my living room.

                    But   the joy
made
when sun promises to come back another again.
                                Maybe it is the face
of   somewhere

a newborn child.
          Or
              The sound of light meets the utopia in my
mind. I don't know what it is   but

tonight.
It feels like   an orchestra playing live
and   g I g a n t I c   in my veins.

Like.
My reason is
here.

And I can only know that because

there is orange and blue outside

your living room, too.
Can't you see?!

I'm trying to say that I love you.
In breath   and   by wonder
for all your sunsets come true.

Regina G. Shepherd

So Much of My Now

So much of my now
        is unlearned togetherness.

When he sits across a table
or some other speaking
        vestibule

He'll ask about habits
                the news
                Shade Room
        and past dalliances.

I'll be able to tell him
                that I'm sure that I know
                sad eyes
and without them
                he is to me
                an unsure strangeness.

How I awake in moments
        hoping that children
                will not have those sad eyes.

Regina G. Shepherd

I remember that potentially my mother my father my brother
looked at me the same one infant day
And I whimper.
And I break. Like orange pulp
under teeth and suckle.

ROBERT REYNOSO (DE LARGO HALEINE)
I Sighed Relieved by Pocket Lint

I sighed relieved by pocket lint

Best to be spending

Locally,

stand steadily

Planning,

planted in place

By choice

Than be moved

swept up by the lucrative swell

of this inevitable wave

Extending up from the southern bush, the bridge

the origins of this foreign catalyst from out of state

Familiar airs but not always the same

But seldom are extremes helpful,

Affluence is not the dirtiest word

not the char in the monochrome spectrum

Especially if more green is used for our shared garden

Especially if more is invested in clean water

to rinse the sanguine earth for everyone who's

mined here

But if the jewels that are surfaced then on
are only for the hands of a novel few to keep
Then know that when they effortlessly gloat,
gleam and sparkle

It's because they are rich in the most tangible
immoral minerals
And that is a dire set of fotos
when that poverty has a long exposure without the flash
Highlighting those underserved structures without the cash
showing a particular stress on the frame
but also, those talents who juggle the struggle
That piece the meal through their honest hustle
Know that your pictures are also deeply rich in detail
your character's resilient fatigues captured
In the golden ratio
Know that our spiritual health is strong
Our history reflected
in the passing of beams
Our lumen glow in the yonder
breaks from vehicles streak
Connote a wider aperture
There's more depth to this field
from which to grow new plants

Robert Reynoso

More hands to carve from mud

More sun and time to craft

mounds to stand and pitch

Advocate for more than lint

Have control

For a better future of different shades

Partner: Freehand Trace

Be with a creative partner
Who can boldly lay outlines to your ebbs and flows
And survive the freehand trace of your sharp peaks
during unprecedented seismographic living

RICHARD WESLEY PICKETT
(RICHARD PIGKASO)
Lets Get Money

Money is the root of all evil.
And evil is just another name of what they call people
From coins, to the paper, to the checks, to the debit cards
Even when you buy nothing feel like you getting charged
Don't need cable because I got that fire stick
hacking my neighbors WiFi yeah you know them wire tricks
Got to sit back and try to save up
Before I start walking these trains now with a change cup
Don't know why God put me in poverty
Wanna get my money clean but itching for a robbery
It really sucks on the daily now being sad and broke
I would tell you it's funny I'm really bad at jokes
The better days will come, can't turn away and run
I over-drafted on my sneakers, I couldn't pay the funds
It's my life now, it's really sad and true
So do you kind of think I'm probably doing just as bad as you
It isn't looking good being black in America
Gentrification is now attacking my area

It's a cryin shame, as you lie in pain

You're gonna leave this world alone and probably die in vain

But I move in silence, so I don't need to shout

I plant my money trees and then you'll see the seeds will

sprout

All over the nation then probably the globe

Just don't be in the rush when you got to see the dough

Give the money to the poor and the hungry

Even to the whites that slam the door and call us monkeys

They do it purposely almost feels like a curse to me

Mother can't feed her starving child it really hurts to see

Walking a straight line I'm on the road to the riches

And I'm waiting for the boat to pass but they control the

bridges

Just wanna chill rest my soul on a beach

Pay attention to moves watch the goals imma reach

What's a bill to the rich that's never known broke

Has enough money to even snort his own coke

Never drove through the ghetto just to see how we living

Hope is coming soon just see the vow is winning

Feeling like everything in the world is dark and grim

Don't blame you little man but you got to start to sin

Cause this is your life it's really sad but true

And to be honest I'm glad I'm not doing as bad as you

BIANCA CLENDENIN

Decaying infrastructure

The greatest city in the world
is on fire.
She already knows
what it's likes to burn.
My parents remember,
the smell still lingers.
Buildings just happen
to light up and smudge
the sky.
A reminder of all
the poor folks
who couldn't fight back
against the housing titans
of their heyday.
New York City is a cinder block,
just waiting for the ticker.
It won't matter if your
home isn't safe
from greedy developers.
Ready to turn your home
of 20 years

Bianca Clendenin

to a shitty cold bulk
for the upper upper-middle
class white yuppy__
Do people still use 'yuppy'?
Or it that just an outdated 80s
"slur"?

For now I drift,
back to what I used to know.
Remembering myself in
familiar places.
Places covered in gold:
gold hoop earrings,
'we sell gold here' signs,
gold crosses adorned on brown necks,
glittery gold shoes dancing
in tiny dark rooms,
and greasy bodega gold
of bacon, egg, cheese on rolls.

Then there's the now
of today.
Places replaced by bricks:

Bianca Clendenin

Overpriced exposed brick bedrooms,
too hip brick coffee shops,
red brick brownstones
hidden on my vision board,
and yellow bikes against
brick buildings ready to
be torn down.

Those cold spaces
with their water down
Scandinavian designs.
Dreaming to be progressive
to be clean lines
and perfection.
But it's a 2 bedroom
disguised as 4.
Walls and walls and walls.
Exposed brick for days.

To get that picture,
imagine my first apartment:
The heart of changing
Bushwick.
A false room,

missing a wall.
Feeling exposed
Feeling exposed
Bricks cost more.
With a window looking
into my neighbor's kitchen.
Feeling exposed
Feeling exposed
Gentrification is costly
and a scam.
That one window brick room
is where I fell in love
but also where I realized
how ugly my city is,
my dying city.

They're pushing us away
not just with high rents
but with increased
subway fares,
ticketed arrests for
jumping turnstiles,
stop and frisk,

funding for
"Specialized"
charter schools,
food deserts,
and the list goes on
and on
and on.

It's a shadow of itself.

Even in my youth,
I knew romanticizing this city
is dangerous.
I love it so.
Love it with my bones.
I'll die here,
without a doubt.
Yet it's crumbling
because too many people
want their dreams
to live out like that
tv show or a movie,
or their fav podcast.
All without a single Black

face in sight.
You know the ones.
I...was born here
Don't I have that right?
To live that impossible dream?

Maybe not.
It's a false dream
on false promises
and decaying love.
Clinging onto
spoon-fed history.
That just might not be
enough anymore.
Drown me in the East River
already.
It will happen in 10 years
anyway
Thanks, Cuomo

YANETTE ROSARIO
Where I'm From

I'm from drums,
From sazón goya and jugo de chinola.
I'm from a small apartment in the
Patterson Housing Projects.
I'm from ordering a baconeggeandcheese
with an arizona ice tea can every morning before school,
From wearing Northface coats and timbs during the winter,
And from eating mango, rainbow, cherry, and coco coquitos
during the summer.

I'm from "it's brick outside",
From A Tribe Called Quest songs blasting from a jeep.
I'm from chasing down the Mr. Softee truck whenever we
hear its jingle,
From getting wet in open fire hydrants,
I'm from freestyling in the park with my friends,
From my aunts' blessings – "Que Dios Te Bendiga".

I'm from the roses that adorn my grandmother's hair,
From the plátano trees that grow in my family's native land.
I'm from dancing loud merengue and bachata,

And from learning how to cook sancocho and morro.
I'm from my father's hard work and mother's perseverance,
From "Mira, un día tienes que ser alguien" and
"Tu educación tiene más valor que el dinero".

I'm from reading at night before bed,
And watching the sunset on summer afternoons,
I'm from the Blackness of my great grandfather,
From yucas and batata,
From my family's migration from a beautiful island to the
concrete jungle,
I'm from where the corners of the world meet.
I am from the South Bronx.

CHRISTOPHER LAING
You

I like you.

I like you?

I like you.

I LIKE YOU!

I...love you

I love...you

I love you...

You loved him?

You loved him.

You loved HIM.

You married him.

But I loved you.

I loved you.

I loved you,

But you loved him.

I liked you,

I loved you,

You loved him.

You married him,

But I loved you.

Crushed.

Christopher Laing

My Love For You

If my love for you is chaos, then I am driven by insanity.
The days I don't see you send me into madness,
But in that madness I am reminded of you.
The soft, slow strokes of your love lift my smile.
Your tender thoughts warm my heart with a love I have never
felt before.
I miss those big, black, curly strands of hair
getting caught in my mouth when we cuddle.
I cherish the times you opened your heart to me
And hate myself for not being entirely open with you.
Our love will blossom again one day.
I hope this message brings you peace
Because my love for you keeps me lost
In blissful chaos.

CHELSEA ROJAS
The Problem of Poverty I

I grew up looking poverty in the face
I knew her name before I knew mine

We lived on the same E 149th Street and
somehow managed to have different lives

Her eyes, so wide, humble and full of life

And I, full of pride, rolled mine from a well kept Chevy and
moved on by
As I saw her book it daily to catch the Bx5

As I grew, she did too

Her hair was coarse, brittle and parted down the middle
Mine was thick, shiny and did a really good job to hide me

Our neighbors never had a problem trying to find me
I was always the girl with the "good hair"
And the family who looked like they cared

Chelsea Rojas

While she was the one that I wouldn't see for days
I would wonder if I should ring her doorbell often
So that she could come down to play

It haunted us, to feel this way
To act like everything was always okay

It's a tragedy, to be born in poverty

You have no mother but I have mine
You have no couch but mine is unoccupied by the ones I love

We claim to speak different languages
But I'm sure Tower of Babel would marvel at how we ended
up sounding the same

Poverty is in my eyes and poverty has worn out your skin
Two tones that have bled the same color
Our wounds have holes the same shape and size as our
wonder of

Is this all I will ever know?

Chelsea Rojas

The Problem of Poverty II

Poverty is pervasive, often portrayed as personal

Only considered a public affair when the pain is pictured on
platforms painted for praise

Poverty shouldn't be a commodity yet profit is made

People aren't property
That's the problem to face

The "poor" that we walk past by, they don't want our pity
They rather we speak
Bring peace to the streets they walk with their bare feet

A safe place to lay
A quiet night without a need to pop a pill and hope the
pounding will go away

A product of "the environment" they say
But we all know it takes a village to raise a child so why do we
look the other way?

Chelsea Rojas

It's the pride that we hide behind
The thoughts that we push aside
The discomfort to actually try

"But what am I supposed to do?"
The same old question can't land on deaf ears again

No more living in pretend that we can't make it end
Even if my President doesn't comprehend

My privilege compels me to speak
How can I stand here with you and not be moved by you?
Enough to do something for you

Whether I pant and pace
I will proclaim the words past generations prayed for me to
now say

And my brothers keeper I will be

Because this isn't all we will ever have to know

JESSICA 'TOMOKO' PÉREZ
Weather Man

When the rain
goes drip, drip, drop
these feelings, they won't stop
this heaviness, won't quit
so I prepare for lift off
-enter a
phase where
gravity don't exist
off my center of balance,
becoming weightless
these feelings they ease up
when I'm in my inner space
the cycles move and shift
but it's ironic
every time I'm heating up
I suddenly get the chills
…sensitive to the cold
cuz the weather just changes

I can't stand this weather, man
I can't stand this weatherman

He's got it out for me

Because even when the clouds diverge
the sun shine a little dimmer than what I remember
got a feeling in my bones... gonna be a long winter
pray to god,
I keep them layers on
lest I stay shivering
in a pile of memories I never got rid of
much ado about nothing
I
got
me
a
whole
agenda

I think I see
the lightning coming
bright
composure
running out
sounds to me a little something like

Jessica 'Tomoko Pérez

some thunder rumbling now

Weatherman,
can you tell me how...
I heard there's pie in the sky
and my head is up in the clouds
got my eyes on the horizon
my energy's in the ground
the air is getting thinner
but Spring's nothing more than a figment
of my imagination
just let me know when the sleet is
coming
to wake me from my dreams
of internal tranquility
the flowers on the ground
don't even look at me, they pity me

JOSUE MENDEZ
Everyday

Eight in the morning
Eighteen passengers
Ate no breakfast yet again

Two minutes, four to the six
Dancing starts: "Showtime!"
Got no time for this

A halting motion,
"Apology for delay"
Another day, late

MORCEY FELIX
Sistah

The soils of plantations prick at my flesh like ticks on the skin
of animals that been unkept
house nigger is what they call me

Pigmentations of rape seasoned my dna
and swaddled my existence
for I am the grenade implanted inside of a slave woman who
embodied strength but feared resistance
because it meant death

Through gritted teeth and splintered feet
I call for you I search for you but these oppressed halls ain't
made for our voices to be heard through
Sistah do you hear me

We have rested in same womb
but invisible barriers keep us at bay
me on the inside and you the forgotten
picking the very thing that keeps American on her limbs
COTTON
Sistah do you feel me

Morcey Felix

Your melaninated skin with blackberry undertones is a
reflection of a place we may never return

to

HOME

and I

I am the reflection of silent cries and bloody thighs
whispers of freedom
Sistah do you see me

It's dark and hell is hot
the trees are burning in Mississippi
the programming has begun
the world says I'm better than you because
I'm the lighter
so we use this fuel and displace the love
allowing the powers that be to always have one up on us
Sistah do you receive me?

Neither one of us has won
only difference is you got the drunk uncle
and I got the sober one
but the aftermath remains
uneven knee highs innocent fruits stained
Sistah do you believe me

Morcey Felix

I can only imagine what the world has put you through
but I would stand here on broken glass
and walk there with you
you see
I would hug the tree bare back and receive every lash that
cause pain for you
all 400 years worth
I would shred every magazine that doesn't display you
and all the men that tried to play you
and said you pretty
for a dark-skin girl
I would take those words and crumble them
through them in the air and reconstruct them
ill tattoo them on your heart
it says
YOU ARE BLACK
YOU ARE BEAUTIFUL
SISTAH, YOU ARE ART

THE BENJAMIN POETS: JANETH BENJAMIN,
EVON BENJAMIN,
& TAVIA BENJAMIN
I am Poetry

I am poetry
I am the poet who finds meaning in the desertion of thought
and life, reckless intellectual abandonment for the sheer
pleasure of literary euphoria, an oasis of omnipotence.
I am poetry,
Angst holding me captive,
I am you
Everything you are afraid to say
Who you are afraid to be
I am the validation of your truth
I am poetry
Breathing dewdrops, releasing thunderstorms, holding your
heart hostage, a mind trapped in voices unspoken, unread,
sprawled over unruled pages, without background music.
I am poetry
smudged ink on worn pages
stained faces with seabound tears
a drenched soul amid the daring sunlight of the ones
we wish saw us

standing rock bound among the ones whose souls connect

like ours ...

with words.

I am... poetry

I am poetry,

The feeling you can't shake

Smothering your consciousness

Impeding your 'normalmess'

Wandering, wanting,

Aching, haunting,

pawning away at your insatiable desire for rest.

JANETH BENJAMIN
Grow Through

People don't expect you to change.
They expect you to be the same person you were last year or
even the year before. They have been so consumed with their
ideas about you that they fail to see pieces of you falling apart.
Pain changes things.
The pain you can't explain
in just one sentence changes everything.
Even after knowing what you've gone through they expect
you to be the same. While you were wading through hell and
high water, battling with yourself about your inhibitions, and
simply trying to stay afloat,
they were wondering why you were acting funny.
Walking roads alone and finding things to help you sleep, just
making sure that tomorrow you will remember to breathe,
they felt that you were angry about something they might
have done. Except, your thoughts were centered around
finding peace,
facing the truth and courageously forgiving yourself.
Working on letting go of the things you can't control and
healing your broken heart, once again. Most importantly,
reconnecting and strengthening your relationship with God.

They didn't see the pieces falling and they didn't see how you put them back together.

Learning to put yourself first, like really put yourself first. Doing things you want to do and yes, doing them alone because you're the best company you will ever have.

Trust me, self-care is the most important job you will have.

Pain changes everything.

Putting yourself first is everything.

There is no going back.

There is no space in your existence for anything or anyone that will constantly take and barely give.

Facing battles alone and knowing exactly how much you are worth leaves no room for mediocrity.

It is amazing how even after keeping your head above water, you still feel like you're drowning and it takes you back to that day but you remember.

You remember, how many days it took and how many tears fell, and how you kept going because you know, you know, that the valley was never meant to break you. God sent reinforcements and you pulled through.

Now you smile; you look back and you smile.

Still, people don't expect you to change.

They want to know what happened but without true understanding, they will never get it.

They don't try to get to know this you, they are still stuck on an idea of you, their idea of you.

Janeth Benjamin

Melanin-Rich

Melanin is rich

Melanin is flavor

Melanin is a rich spice, underrated yet, desired

The variety you heard about

The variety you need

Flavor

Chocolate, caramel, coconut, rich

Melanin is sweet

fresh sugar cane sweet, no fertilizer, no preservatives

Thirst quencher on a hot sunny day, sweet

Melanin is fire

Cayenne, Scotch Bonnet, bird pepper fire

No water can cool this fire

But you like the burn

The sass, the wit, the charm

Melanin is cinnamon

soothing, calming, close your eyes and inhale the richness

thighs, no thighs, hips, no hips, curved lips, happy nappy,

twists, and curls

curvy, not curvy

Cut from a different cloth

Variety

Janeth Benjamin

The variety you heard about
The spice you need
Melanin
Melanin-rich

MIQUEAS R. MOLANO
Permission

Let me sew your lids to the nape of your neck and to the
bottom of your double chin.
Let me chew on your teeth,
Taste my seasoned journey.
Let me dirty your bleached brain with my spectrum of hues.
Let my international tongue
Bang on your drum
Feel the rhythm your color lacks.
Let me walk with my hat backwards
Around my neighborhood without
My neighborhood calling the badge
To pull me aside
Like I displaced their sense of safety from their palms.
Let me enjoy a drive down the street with Hector, Celia,
Anthony, Toño, Nicky y Fefita.
Déjame tener una conversación
Que tú no puedes entender
Porque tú no te críaste como traductor
Para tus padres.
Let me look back at your atrocities as they are.

So I can know why I'm your leper.

So I can know why you think you stand higher than me.

So I can know why I ask you to let me do the things you've

continuously done without

Permission

NAOMI FIGUEROA

Dissension

I wonder if I'll be the second one in your story.
Unashamed
Guilty of running away from these feelings
until my thread buckled
And sent me hurdling backwards.
I wish I could say I felt something.
Rattling questions of a list
Yes and No.
Tossing out the same question
My heart should of been beating faster, love?
It's still love, right?
You're right, yes, it's possible,
More than possible, it's a reality in my mind
I'm grinding my teeth to hide my smile
Don't smile. This is not happiness.
It is bitter, sour, bloody- almost bruised
Your voice bounced off the walls
My hands wanting to fly up to my ears.

In all earnest truth
I just want this to be over.

I just want you to shut the door.
I want so badly to cry at the right moments.

But my heart keeps leaping out of my chest
at the sound of his name,
I had to grip my pillow tightly from the fear that you'd see it.
What I'm capable of just for him.
No, you'd never understand.
You are not a wildfire.

You are a soft stream.
You still do not know what it is like when thunder strikes.

Naomi Figueroa

Rapture//Rupture

I have learned a thousand ways to romanticize destruction.

So now,

When

I

Fall

Apart

I know.

Here comes a beautiful feeling…

MARIO A. REYES

Castles in the Clouds

Ayo

Look around and tell me what you see

I see castles kissing the curves of clouds at the northern most point of New York City

My block is unique

Its so unique it's not even called a block it's a loop because you gotta make that U every time you come thru

I am Co-op City

And I mean that whole heartedly because Co-op has the whole heart in me

And if you were raised here you know that statement isn't hard to see

I mean we had it goooood....

How many babies in the eighties were raised around safety

My building was considered the village that raised me

From Nancy to James and always Ms. Daisy

To the way we knew better than to run thru the Jews

Mario A. Reyes

In front of the building sun bathing

So we went to the back,

That's where you earned your stripes slap boxing,

We ain't even have sand boxes we had sand blockses

Lost in the sands of time,

so from the windows our parents watched us

or sat on the last terrace on the roof

Ask Ajene..

The things we did,

The innocence that this neighborhood afforded its kids,

Even without scratch there was always PAL and YAC,

Steve knew we ain't have but we promised to pay him back,

Trusted us enough to give a 9 year old a tab,

The good humor, man taught me about credit!?

Where else would u find this

Lost in the sands of timeless

And every time I visit I'm somehow reminded

please don't mistake my reminisces with disses

The residences are a mere shell

with out the residents within it,

We had legends

From every section,

My personal favorite was Sammy,

His wit was uncanny with God given intelligence

My address was 120 but he kept it 100

whenever he was questioned,

because honesty always inspires good intention

Ayo I'm so Co-op I use to shop at rickles!!

I'm serious I remember when Bay Plaza wasn't even there..

I'm so Co-op a yardy

sold me a Tommy shirt at the flea market,

had me gasses it was official...

My block said it was fake and I was wack,

So the next week I went back

and stole a pair of jeans to match

I'm so Co-op I snuck into the movies on a first date in the back,

I'm so Co-op I went to 153, 180 and Truman,

I'm so Co-op I remember when traffic on Bartow was moving,

I am killah curve, St Michaels church, Capies and Seven Seas,

I am Buddah Park, Ninja Forest, the plaza,

and Bellamy

I am unique because all of these names ring within me,

I say proudly rest in peace to Marly, Sammy, Lamar, Harrigan, and my big brother Corey,

And

dead ass I've been to the four corners of this world...

After they get a load of me

They ask me where I'm from,

I say Q4 - Co-op City!!!

And they say huh?

They ask where's that;

Mario A. Reyes

I say Da Bronx!!!

They say they never heard of it,

I say you'll never forget it if you not scared to ride along,

Now right or wrong,

In our youth I see greatness

Endowed with gifts they just lament

No more activities so they pound the pavement

If you take anything from this poem,

let it be this statement...

I implore you all not to fight amongst sections

because that was our biggest failure

5 fingers tight are stronger in your hand

So imagine how 5 sections United with a plan can inspire a
movement that starts at home but is felt across lands

That's why wolves run in packs

So be a trail blazers and let the world follow our tracks,

Facts...

Mario A. Reyes

Now I want everyone to look around and tell me what you
see,

I see nothing but love,

so show each other some for my community

We are Co-op and its a beautiful thing to be,

Not gutter, just unique

I promise u I'm so Co-op my name is still tagged in one of
these 35 buildings...

Shhhhhhhhh, lol

SHEVONE ADAMS

Hip Hop

The Bronx

Hip Hop's Mother

There will never be another

Child who can encompass

Highs and lows of lie

In a rhythm that's a highlight

For the young and bold

Who hear their stories told

FAITH BROWN
SUNDAY
MOURNING
WAITING
ASPHYXIATING

Sunday morning, early early morning, three a.m. in the morning, my amen in the morning, I am mourning.

I am mourning my lost emotions, displaced from my head and hands. I've casted them away to face the bustle of everyday normality.

So early Sunday morning, I am waiting, asphyxiating.

I am waiting for my starved sentiments to surface again, to reach these hands, so the reader can feel them with their own. So the reader can learn from my poems, feel from my poems, escape the everyday normality or face the everyday normality, can relate their everyday normality to my poems.

And in turn I do the same with others.

Sunday morning, early early morning, three a.m.in the morning, my amen in the morning, I am looking for poetry, for people's lost emotions to define my own, align with my own. Especially regarding what is now considered my everyday normality, our everyday normality.

Everyday is deranged, insane, demented and it's only getting worse. With poetry, we can trace these crazy, happy, and sad realities that has become our everyday normality and make a mark in the world to touch others. We need this poetry, that yearns to touch the truth.

Our poetry can be displayed in a case, untouchable to the outsiders because they just won't understand.

Our poetry can be hung from a banner over it all, omniscient, presenting to everyone what just is. Our poetry can be sprayed on a dull wall, masked but determined to unmask meaning to us all.

Our poetry can be pressed into cement—permanent.

Our poetry can be caressed into sand, only to remain for a short duration so the message can fade but continue on to be carried on into the waves.

At least it will touch someone.

Don't we need this?

Poetry that can mirror our everyday normality?

Poetry where you can hear the yearn in words that others may not be able to speak or even utter?

Poetry that heals the loss you may be yearning
or mourning for?

Faith Brown

Sacrifice

The man
with the pajama pants
his perfect
patterned
symmetric squares
dance
as he steps
through the train.

Everyone
turns away
anticipating his
chant
in English
then Spanish
he ends
"Bendiciones
a todos."

Discrete
in the corner seat
his pungent perfume

Faith Brown

like apple cedar vinegar
detoxes me
from my fantasy
to this reality.

A woman gives him
a dollar or two
he smiles
missing teeth,
the white coating
on his tongue
creeps through
"God bless you."

My eyes shift back
to his soft sheep wool
as he continues
getting closer
brown spots
appear
and get darker
like blood clots

"I'm sorry"

Faith Brown

is all I say
and he smiles
teary eyed
brunette tangled hair
like Jesus Christ
"God bless you."

Pepsi

On Edwards Avenue
of The Bronx
Pepsi
would stand
tall and slim

bright spandex
short shorts,
a cropped white tank top
painted onto his
bronzed skin

colored stripes
on a stick
hanging from his hip.

"Call me Pepsi"

The summer air
was
stagnant and thick
like syrup

Faith Brown

whiffs of iron lingered
from our casual
open wounds

but our communal wheels
continued gliding through the
neighborhoods
glossed water
rushed over
the fire hydrant's
crud and rustiness.

He
sometimes addressed as she
would smile
his
eye wrinkles
would spread like wings

he'd hand out skinny 99cent ices
and we'd tear the tough plastic
with our teeth

strawberry, cherry, lime, grape, blueberry

Faith Brown

flavors
dripping from our chins
staining our jeans.

COACH TEA

The whole family is incarcerated

It's not even therapeutic anymore.

It's mandatory.

Necessary.

Not even fun no more.

Feeling like a robot.

Much Love.

Hold your head.

We miss you.

These phrases come from my pores.

I am used to it now.

Writing.

5 letters.

20 letters.

40 letters.

Letter after letter.

Brother after Brother.

Mother after Mother.

The WHOLE family is incarcerated.

Incarcerated Heroes

I remember calling him when I was afraid,

alone or felt violated.

He showed up. He showed out. I felt safe.

Please don't mess with me; I don't want to have to call Sal.

Don't make me call Sal.

Damn I wish I could call Sal.

Now – he is amongst the incarcerated heroes.

The ones that were brave enough to fight back.

Protect their families.

Hit back their abusers.

Rise against resistance.

They showed up. They showed out. They kept us safe.

INCARCERATED HEROES.

MIOSOTTY HICIANO
Smoke

Is he making his exit

Or am I Interrupting

Does he think he can exit me

He knows the answer

it comes easily

With that being said

The rest is a mess

A complete lack of interest

I don't feel respect

Take it or leave it

But I know you won't leave it

That look in the car

said that u need it

Confused

Got in a haze

Gone a couple months

And now I'm the haze

I smoke almost everyday

Still can't see you

Am I high enough?

Miosotty Hiciano

Do I meet your standards

Seems like this is tough
Your opinion of me definitely has changed you
Your attitude has changed me

2nd to nothing
I know I mean something
Figure it out
Trying to make me feel a way
Still I try
Still I already died

ARGENIS TAVERAS

Waterproof

Below the bustling roar of the overhead subway station that runs above 167th Street and River Ave is a large gathered crowd of about sixty people. They're closely huddled at the corner of the street block, partially protected from the light rain under the green awning of a local pharmacy. With the sky gray and dark, the cluster of people are illuminated by pink orbs that flash around the word *OPEN*, the burning yellow of electric candles before them, and the blue light emitted by a nearby LinkNYC kiosk made completely of glass. "Crime reduced by 60 percent in the last fifteen years," reads the kiosk before switching to another fact.

"Juno, brother, you left too soon," says Justice. She's delivering a speech in front of the mural of a young, brown face as the crowd watches around her. The flash of their smart phones and of the floating spherical cameras belonging to news stations lend a holy glow not just to Justice's face – which sheds salty drops indistinguishable from those of the falling drizzle – but to the four-foot face of Juno. It stares down at the crowd with a perfect white smile, one complemented by the twinkling of its hand-painted eyes and

charming demeanor. Above its black, curly locks is a ring
painted in a shimmery metallic gold. A ribbon with
2020-2037 written on it hangs underneath the neck.

"How long will we have to endure this type of violence
in our own backyards?" Justice continues as she stares at the
electric candle in her hand. "The blood of our young brothers
runs through these streets like rain in the gutter. When will
we learn? Juno was just seventeen, on his way home from a
friend's house." She looks up from the glass bulb shaped to
look like a flame and scans the body of people for the face of
her mother, whose sullen expression remains calmer than
those around her. "My mother Maria is here," Justice tries
through a cracked voice. "She raised us with the Bible in
hand to show us right from wrong. She attended all our
parent-teacher conferences, cooked us dinner every night.
She kept us away from the streets and away from the gangs.
And Juno was the most innocent of us all, a scholar with
dreams. So why? Why should such an innocent soul have to
fear walking through the streets of his own neighborhood,
having lived here all his life? What does it say about us as a
community that a kid can't walk around here without having
to peer over street corners to make sure he doesn't meet the
same end as my brother? That he can't take out his cell for a

second without it attracting the attention of blood hungry thugs? A phone. My brother's gone over a phone…"

Justice places the candle down to join it with the hundreds of others lined up by the mural. Despite their supposed ability to resist it, a few of the bulbs flicker after hours of exposure to the sky's fallen wetness. *These cheap waterproof things*, Justice thinks. *How ironic that everything is cheap and waterproof, but bulletproof things are so expensive to make. After all, what can a bullet stop? A heart? Water can devastate entire nations. And if the glass my brother stood behind was bulletproof, he'd still be here.*

After setting it down, Justice walks over to a round, gray device that floats centimeters above the dampened pavement. LEDs that shoot short skyward streams of white lasers line its circumference. She tiptoes to the ON button to activate the lasers, making sure to not step over the hundreds of electronic roses that fill the gaps of space between each electronic candle. Doing so will crush the thin tubes that run along their stems and petals, tubes that resemble a natural rose's veins and that pulse with a bright crimson light. Like the candles, the lasers flicker before aligning themselves at specific angles, coordinated in such a way that they create a 3D model of Juno as a toddler.

"Tonight, we remember you, Juno. We commemorate who you are and who you were supposed to be." As Justice speaks, the 3D model slowly morphs to show Juno aging with snapshots of important moments – graduations, birthday parties, championship games. "But we must also remember the hundreds of other innocent kids in the history of this city that shared the same unfortunate fate as you after being in the wrong place at the wrong time. You'll live on in the memory of these streets and in our hearts," Justice finishes.

The lasers begin to move in a way that resembles video playback, displaying security footage of Juno's final moments. It shows him running away from his alleged killers and entering a local pharmacy with a green awning on the corner of 167th and River. But before Juno could duck behind a counter or hide behind a shelf of greeting cards, bullets fly in through the single automatic door, shattering it to shards before reaching their intended target. The crowd watches in dreary silence and fail to flinch from having already seen the video make its rounds on social media. The gray floating device ends its light show by extending the lasers to a height of multiple stories, re-coordinating themselves to shine Juno's face in the sky.

All of the Bronx will be mourning tonight.

Cion Mami'

I'm lying in bed, stuffed underneath layers of blankets. This Washington Heights apartment is old, so if you wish to stay warm, you must use the heat from both the pole that runs from the floor to the ceiling, and layers upon layers of insulating fabric. The air that slips in from slight cracks in my window-frame provide a pleasing contrast between the toastiness circulating in my cocoon and the frost that lingers just outside of it.

Even from under here, I can hear silverware clashing against each other in the kitchen. I can hear utensil drawers being opened and closed, and I can hear the sloshing of the faucet's stream running against plates. The sound comes from my mother, who on this brisk yet sunny Saturday morning is already in the kitchen preparing breakfast for her children. The sound of the metals hitting each other do their part in waking me up. It's an annoying sound, but I recognize it accompanies the preparation of a traditional Dominican breakfast made with a mother's unconditional love.

It's not long before I can hear the ripping of tough platano skin. I can track my mother's movements with just her sound and my knowledge of the apartment layout. I can hear — no, feel — her walk to the kitchen trash can and use her foot to step on the lever that opens it, before discarding the platano skin. I can feel her walk a couple feet back to the front of the sink, tiny sonic booms left in her wake from the slapping of her flip flops against the heel of her foot and the tiled kitchen floor. She turns one of the stove's burners and its iconic initial clicks permeate the apartment before igniting itself. She fills up a pot with water and slams it against the top of the stove. After washing the platano, she drops them into the pot. *Bloop bloop bloop bloop.*

My favorite part of this concert is the cheering. Upon making contact with a hot oil-smeared pan, multiple sliced salami hiss a smoky applause. It's as if the salami is congratulating itself on being delicious salami. A few seconds of cooking and its aroma drowns the house.

l was already woken up, but now I'm driven to actually get out of bed. I toss my legs over its edge, slipping my feet into flip flops bearing a distinct combination of red, white, and blue with the holy book of Catholicism in the middle. God, patriotism, and liberty.

As I walk out of my bedroom and into the living room, I'm greeted by tiny statues of Saint Mary littered across the apartment. One rests on the stand by the television, others on tiny shelves nailed into the wall beside paintings of fruit.

Sunlight coming in from the windows hit the plastic covers on our couches. The plastic has a mind of its own; always making quiet rubbing sounds without anyone sitting on it. I touch a cross nailed near the apartment front door. I've made it my own tradition to rub it every morning just so I can feel close to Papa Dios.

"*'Cion Mami,*" I say groggily to my mother.

"*Que Dios te bendiga,*" she kisses my forehead back and serves me my breakfast.

KEISHA MOLBY-BAEZ

Intuition Doesn't Lie

Two mountains

A fault line

A cliff

Polished black stone

Falling into a pit

A hidden cemetery

Significance lost to time

The soil is moist

Roots of young trees

The sky is grey

The air full of fog

Blurry patterns

A log over a river

Pathway to heaven

A tunnel under the bridge

Doorway to hell

Intuition leads

Sunlight lit the way

Dark entity created a void

Inner voice saved the day

MIA ESTEVES
For Lack of Energy

For so long I fed off of those around me.
Somewhere along the way,
I was led to believe that
I ~~needed~~ you.
Despite the lack of nutrients
I was ~~content~~.
But I've come to realize
That the taste of my own energy
Is far better than your scraps..

Mia Esteves

Spitting Image

I have a bad habit of allowing others
to greatly influence my emotions.
Constantly consuming people like a pill,
Searching for an escape,
A never ending need to get high.
Poisoning myself in the long run
Because just like the effect of drugs,
people are *temporary*.
& I get attached.

I'm scared of ending up just like my mom.
Addicted, depressed and *lonely*.
I fiend for presence, acknowledgement, connection.
Desperately holding on to something
that is no longer there.
Clinging to things I know are no good,
Because to me, it is better than nothing.
Stuck in this never ending nightmare &
It is me, that I am trying to save myself from.

In a lot of ways, I <u>AM</u> my mother.

Mind Control

I've always wondered why
people stayed in controlling relationships
F*ck that!
You got the wrong one!
You're not gonna beat up on me and think it's ok!
Not me!

But no one ever warned me about the abuse
that hits deeper than what the eye can see
See, I never saw beyond the physical
Until he was the reason why I decided to shrink myself
and turned to self inflicted pain
to rid myself of this disdain

I too have been a victim of domestic violence
Forced to keep silent
Shrinking and shifting
to fit your needs
Terrified of simply being me

Constantly asking myself,
but aren't I who you fell in love with?

And yet you're the one who makes me wish
that I had something tangible to be able to claim
and since I didn't, I thought it was okay to stay

You were good like that
Making me lose track
of who caused the problem
You never needed to raise a hand
or a voice to get what you wanted
You always made me think that
somehow I deserved it

I was over here pitying those
who were being controlled
Meanwhile,
that's all I've ever known

MELISSA AMAYA

Bronx Rebel

When I was fifteen years old I skipped class religiously. High school was brutal. The fact that it's even considered to be a learning institution is laughable. One day sophomore year, I over hear these girls in my class talk about getting tattoos. They mentioned a shop on 125th called Aces.

I've always been drawn to body modifications. Which doesn't surprise me seeing as it has been a tradition that has existed among many cultures throughout the world. I knew I had to check this shop out for myself. The next day I skipped my last two classes and headed to Harlem. I convinced my closet friend Janice to tag along for moral support. We entered the establishment and found five men of varying races and ages inside. They stared down at us: two obvious minors all of 5 foot nothing, gripping our backpacks. I stepped forward and asked "how much for 'Bronx' here?" and I pointed to my left hip. They looked back up at each other silently considering it. Suddenly, one spoke up, "Forty." I sucked my teeth, "Nah, thirty-five." "Is this kid serious?" I heard someone say. I glance over at Janice who was timidly standing by the door and gave her a knowing wink. It was a done deal.

Melissa Amaya

I could tell these guys were both shocked and impressed. How often does a teenage girl storm into a tattoo shop demanding a discount on tattoos? Out of respect for my boldness they gave it to me. Thirty minutes later I had 'Bronx' permanently etched into my side and I was loving it. That being said, I would need to hide this for the next three years until I went off to college. If my Roman Catholic Dominican mother saw I had gone behind her back to get a tattoo it would be 'lights out' for me. Every morning before leaving the house she would kindly remind me, "You better not come back to this house with nothing you ain't leave with!" By that she meant tattoos, piercings, and pregnancies, so far I had 2 out of 3. What could I say? In a world where I had such little control, these body mods were a way I was able to claim my body as my own.

I still admire my body mods and they are not something I've grown to regret. Every tattoo, every piercing, and every scar is an emblem of who I was and what I once found important. My Bronx tattoo has faded a little now, but remains one of my favorites. I was a head-ass little bitch back then and I am one now. I will always have pride in being Bronx raised. My ma already has our burial plots bought at St. Raymond's in Throngs Neck. Born, bred, and dead baby. My 'Bronx' tattoo is a reminder of a time in my youth when I knew what I wanted and wasn't afraid to demand it. For too long I allowed my self-image to be dictated by the negative comments of my mother, my family and classmates. It took a lot of work to finally realize that the whole time I was the shit.

Despite the love I have from my mother now and the relationship we have built, she's always been one of my biggest haters. Whether it was my hair, the music I listened to, the way I dressed, these are just a few of the things about me that she disapproves of and she sure as hell makes her opinion voiced. As an immigrant, she has always felt the pressure to assimilate and she pushed that onto me--Don't be loud, don't stand out, just be "una nina normal, una nina desente." From a young age, I never understood why it was abnormal for people to live their truth. Why are people so afraid of a woman who is unapologetically herself? I refused to be small or fit in, I wanted to shine like a disco ball. I have spent most of my adult life unlearning the lies that were beaten into me. These are the same lies that were told to my mother and to the black and brown people for ages.

My ancestors had their own faith before the colonizers showed up bringing their religion and diseases. I have been trying to find my way back to that pure form, but "Catholic guilt" is a heavy boulder weighing on my chest. It's odd, while I do not ascribe to that religion, the chains it has left on me since childhood are not fully broken yet. I wonder if they ever will be. I try to forgive mi mama for the pain she has caused me. Years pass by, and I have realized the reason for her behavior is due to her own personal experiences in this country. Her limited English skills has always left her feeling unsafe and at a disadvantage in Amerikkka. The act of her perming my hair and teaching me to stay silent was her method of protecting me from the cruelties inflicted on brown and black children who dare to be free. Seeing things through her perspective makes it a little less painful. I remind myself that her actions were coming from the internalization her own hurt and fear. I am healing from generational traumas and facing new ones every day, it is fucking exhausting.

Ten years later, at 25, my life looks mad different than it did back then. I am decorated with many tattoos and piercings. My hair is in locs as a refusal of European standards of beauty and as a homage to my ancestors. I am everything my mother feared I would be, I am loud, crude, and hairy. I do not care about making white people uncomfortable because conflict is where the strongest growth happens. My mom has come a long way but she still calls me "pelo malo" and comments when I get "too much sun." She wants me to shave my armpits and find some stability, whatever that means. As a first generation Afro-Latina I fear she will never truly understand me. Honestly, I often wonder if she even wants to and that's what hurts me the most. All I can do is love her for where she is in her own unique journey.

If I could meet my younger self, I would delicately hold her tiny face in my hands. I'd kiss her cheeks and the scars on her wrists. I would tell her that silence will never protect her. One day she will be free to live her truest form. I would let her know that being kind and loving to yourself despite any imperfections is a beautiful act of rebellion. When you live authentically you are telling white supremacy to go fuck itself, that you will never be colonized. Drop the toxicity and people who do not help you become the best version of yourself. Your self-esteem does not stem from how desirable you are to others. The only person who is guaranteed to be in your life forever is you, so you might as well put your energy into becoming a person you're proud of. Before you say something negative to yourself think, 'would I say this to my best friend?' If the answer is 'no' then never say it to yourself! The same love and forgiveness we pass onto others must be reciprocated to ourselves. Please keep your head up baby girl. It is because of your resiliency that we survive and return to the Bronx--with pride in our heart, and on our hip.

VC

Love Is…

Love is a wishing well

Love is your hottest hell

Love is wanting to excel and prevail

but doubtful that what you love

loves you on the same scale

Love is not knowing up from down, left from right

surrounded by darkness yet seemingly finding light

Love makes the best of you

while dragging you through the worst of you

wondering if this is a blessing or a curse for you

So many lessons through

obsession and a search for you

A desert full of feelings and

I'm just dying of thirst for you

See

Love is not a stop, it's a pathway

Pain will come don't be giving in halfway

We believe love is a dance, to the sweetest of serenades

But it's more of a chiseled art,

so let's admire what we've made

STEPHANIE JANECEK
The Streets Alive

The music pours from fourth floor windows
And down the alley
On East 134th Street.
The other side of the bridge.
Horns and wood cover the air
In an updraft of tempo,
The thunder of bass string,
And drum deluge.
I open the window to absorb the scene.
The streets
Set to Music.
A soundtrack to the life
In this place and time.
Traffic and people,
Moving,
Oblivious to the landscape
They decorate so beautifully.
The smooth flow sways into my kitchen.
My alley side window
Views the pluck and blow away performance
Just for me

Stephanie Janecek

Or anyone else who happens
To be listening
Or watching the streets alive
During a Monday's Eve
Late summer jam session.

KRYSTINA ALPHONSO (TEACHA)
UNNERVED

You are unnerved

Among the nervous

That's flamboyantly annoying

Swing your authority like a yoyo

Bounce your nightstick like a pogo

Break open the piñata

The insides of a boy

from my alma mater

Red liquids

Not a kool aid for his daughter

His

Medulla Oblongata

Sacrifice the holy

Drink up all the water

Redistribute the pipes

So now there's lead up in my agua

Come to my town

And get scared of the iguanas

And the lizards

But not the snakes

How can you be scared,

Krystina Alphonso

when you look you in the face?

Huh, Jake?
Huh, flake?
You fucking corny
You be frosted
Force to force it
Call a team of murderers a force
But what the cost is?
I'm talkin bout
the overseers
the officers, who have to stay in office
Administrative duty
for the copper of the plea
who lost it
When he begged thee
To step off like two or three
Not talkin bout the ones
that be out there
tryna save the world
I know no one is perfect
So stop killing boys and girls
It has a ricochet effect
Look at the mass shootings

Krystina Alphonso

The whole country sees you do it
And look who gets influenced
look who get influenced
See I been getting to it
I'm just tryna influence
creators to create
Inspire the BeBe's to debate
But look at the mass shootings
The whole country see you do it

And look who get influenced

Krystina Alphonso

Who am I? Who are you?

Will I become dependent
On an addiction I am spending?
It's all conflicting I can't mend it
If it's a vixen then it's trending ...
My eyes haven't deceived me
Media makes amazing cases
For capitalizing on certain races
Wait wait wait a minute
Race can't be a factor
cuz it's supposed to be fair
So I've erased it from my vision
With my
big
fucking
magical
pencil

Boom.

"I don't see color"
You don't see me,
or them

Krystina Alphonso

or yourself
Keeps you less guilty
and
with no accountability
If it snows
you gone let in ya peeps
While I'm out in the Cold
you expect to get project heat
The shit is broke
Hace frio
It's bricker than
what New York slang can afford
I don't got a ford
I got what I afford
A monthly metro card
Screaming to let me out the back door
You "ain't moving"
Unless niggas move back
Since niggas staying black
Since niggas' funding lacks
You ain't get paid by the rack
At
where you constantly
feel under attacked

Krystina Alphonso

Been in your bodega for years
Never said nothing bout the cat
Cuz in this big city
Gotta keep away the rats
Gotta keep away the racks
Hide em in your favorite slacks
My favorite ones got the dog on em
Cuz if niggas fuck with me
Ima put the paws on em
Ima hit that play
then Ima put the pause on em
Runnin round seeing red
Hit you and the record button
But
I'm from Brooklyn
So I rap a lot
Never pack the gat
Rap's guillotine
Make you gag
like lance a lot

JONATHAN 'THIRDEYESHOOTER' BROWN
Moments of maddening attraction

Cascading in these mistakes
Decisions you've made
Creating greater space
Switching gears, leaving you here.
Feelings became felt
Love became doubt
It's you I don't need to be around.
Cleaning my pallet, you were just residue.

Destroyed by the words you speak
Aiming at your foes while you stare at me
Foreign policies that belittle me.
Crude tools used to elude a fool that loves you
Not too fond of other people fondling you

Think before you speak.
You look meek when you fumble with your speech.
Wouldn't have to be heartless, if you had more thought miss.
And that'll be written in cursive when you are cursing at the
next person.
Gave 100, settled for 15th best I have words on my chest.

Jonathan 'Thirdeyeshooter' Brown

In chess you left me on check,
and I'm leaving you with all the rest.
No change just new names.
I am a bridge, you are water.
I'm so over you.

RICARDO SANTOS
Rich Port

Abuela was born in Puerto Rico around 1942. You could never be too sure with their birthdates. I know of a few people who were born in the islands, either Puerto Rico or the Dominican Republic, and they don't know their birthday. She never spoke much about her days in Puerto Rico, but I never asked her why. She used to have one picture from Puerto Rico in our family album. It was wrinkled, black and white and she has one of the few smiles I had ever seen on her face. She sat in a decorative chair looking into the camera, her eyes youthful and vibrant. Two hands put a white crown on her head, her hair short but well done. There were few people in the background of the picture but no one paid her any mind. A queen lonely at her throne.

She touched down onto the Bronx soil when she was 17 years old. Their first apartment was on 168th Street and Trinity Avenue. She came with her mother, our great-grandmother, who died before we could ever get to know her. Abuela didn't talk about her much either; she held on to her flickering flame of her memory with a single wallet size picture. It was discolored and worn; with a single date written on the back. Her hair was dark gray and white; it was not styled and laid flat against her face. Her eyes were dark and unquestionably tired. Her skin was wrinkled and seemingly hung from her facial bones. Her neck leaned forward and her shoulders slumped against the background curtain. Her shirt was patterned and unbuttoned at the collar. The shirt looked too big and her pants too small. She looked battered; life had taken its fair share of home run swings at her. She couldn't keep score anymore.

Abuela kept it tucked on the corner of her mirror in her bedroom, the picture never moved. It was a constant reminder of what they had gone through; and a peek into her a possible future life. But Abuela was too vibrant and loved Barcadi too much for that shit. She hung it there, but that picture would never be her mirror image.

She witnessed police brutality; she saw her fellow Puerto Ricans and Bronx natives mistreated and ostracized. She always said she never understood why they were so silent; she said maybe they didn't know their rights. Maybe they were too scared; maybe the heat of a bullet was enough to silence the frosty nature of cultural assimilation. The true meaning of the old Bronx Cheer.

Abuela wasn't alone for long. In three weeks after her arrival, her two younger sisters and her brother arrived to the Bronx. The three of them moved in with Abuela and their mother. Her father was a mystery. No one knew where he was. Shit, I never even heard her talk about him. He was such a mysterious figure I always wondered if my great grandmother had her children via the Immaculate Conception. Fathers were always some kind of surreal figure to most people like us. We would see them a handful of times and each moment you would just stare at them; wondering where they had gone. Questioning whether they would ever come back. They were strong enough to fight it; they all went to school for a short period of time, but that didn't last long. Neither did Abuela's single status.

He was rather dark for a Puerto Rican. Without question he was short, but strong willed and closed minded. Abuelo was already here in the Bronx by the time he met her. He was a young superintendent for a dilapidated building over on Grant Avenue. His smile was charismatic and could light up the basement of the apartment that he lived in. He had a thick mustache that hung over his thin lips and his hair was straighter than 9:15 on the clock. Moms used to tell us that it was only that straight because he didn't want the world to know that he was more Moreno than Spaniard. He hated his dark skin and his coarse, curly hair. Abuelo was hiding. They met at a party on the Grand Concourse; he sent her a barcadi rum and coke in a small plastic cup. She accepted it out of courtesy rather than interest. He wore a pair of brown bell bottoms that were too tight around his flat Puerto Rican ass and were ball busters in the front. His polyester shirt was opened at the top collar; too bright and big for his frail body. His platform shoes were black and hard. The heel was over three inches high; hiding in plain sight. After about seven or eight of those small cups of rum, they were dancing salsa in the middle of the living room.

There was no love affair, no dates at the Botanical Gardens or strolls on Orchard Beach. Only a pissed off mother who wondered aloud what was her sixteen year-old daughter thinking. Abuela found herself on the outside looking in; her mother didn't exactly tell her to leave, but she didn't show her enough support for her to stay. So she packed her small amount of clothing and the last of her teenage innocence and left the house with her marido, as her mother used to call him, only two weeks into their crazy courtship. She moved into his basement apartment and found a small space to store her stuff. The apartment, if you want to call it that, was built for a single, drinking callejero who didn't give a fuck if the space around the toilet had piss stains. But she made it work. With her growing belly, she picked up after him and cooked small dinners that he rarely seemed to appreciate. The bigger the belly got, the more he was in the streets drinking. He stumbled his way home and when he found that his pollo wasn't warm and the rice wasn't soft enough he erupted into a rage. He yelled, he screamed; his words resonating so much that the baby in her belly felt the wrath. She didn't want to fight back; she couldn't.

She apologized as much as her pride would allow her to. But when he called her a pendeja and said she wasn't worth the ground she stood on, she lashed back. She slammed the lukewarm plate onto the small, makeshift dinner table. The last of the chicken legs rattled off the plate and dropped to the ground. He pushed Abuela into a wall and she fell. When she collapsed, her water broke. Alone and battered, she walked to the hospital and she pushed and continued to push with all of her strength.

Even as abuelo smacked her face daily, she continued to love him; spawning two more daughters and a baby boy. Abuelo's space was too tight and he couldn't hide anymore. He couldn't handle it anymore; his hands lost control more and more as his family grew older. He tried to hide from them, never realizing that the eyes that tried to watch him loved him more than he ever thought. He moved them from Grant Avenue to Cypress Avenue feeling an avalanche of agony.

When he couldn't hold his job as the super, the once scattered flurry of fights snowballed out of control. But she had enough. Abuela had enough of his booze filled battery; enough of short changing her children with tattered clothes and shoes too small that my aunts' feet would bleed when she walked. No more waking up the next morning, cleaning her nose and the room reeking of booze and an oppressive mix of cheap cologne and Avon perfume.

Abuela was done.
No more wiping tears from faces.
No mas.
Her turbulent flight was finally over, as she finally landed on St. Ann's Avenue.

What a blessing.

Elizabeth Roldan

ELIZABETH ROLDAN
Mother (Personal Essay)

We were told to clear out my late mother's apartment as soon as possible, as the cooperative board said rent would continue to be charged as long as personal possessions remained behind. Despite the fact that my mother had just died from kidney failure one week earlier, I arrived, together with friends, ready to close the book on this last, sad chapter for good. Her apartment looked like it was stuck in a time warp from the mid-90's, what with tape cassettes, long, flat cameras, VHS tapes and other sundry items – junk -- from a time long passed with no historical value. I ended up keeping only her china set and glassware, individual pieces of which stuck to their shelves, so firmly had they remained in place over the past 15 years. Mounds of paper were everywhere, as though not a single document had been discarded for this same duration, as well.

My mother had been diagnosed with cirrhosis of the liver, chronic arthritis, COPD, and had been in and out of rehab for drug and alcohol addiction for some time. She had been very sick, and there were bottles of medications everywhere. Yet she was merely 55 years old, with teeth implants. This made me feel guilty; she'd loved my teeth

BX Writers 272

because they were straight and white, the result of orthodontia she'd taken me for when I was 11 years old.

I found her homework dated from May 1992 from LaGuardia Community College, from which she'd never finished her degree. There were workbooks from a nurse's aide program she'd started but didn't complete. I felt guilt, again, that her own dreams never materialized at the price of my own, as I'd gone on to college, with her support, and attended graduate school at Georgetown University. My graduation pictures decorated her walls. In 2006 my mom and grandmother had flown to Washington, D.C., to help me move for grad school, and it was a trip she'd enjoyed very much. She'd not flown in 6 years, and I remember when I picked her up at the airport he had a huge smile on her face. This was her only excuse for a "vacation" – to see me – while I'd already travelled to Europe, the Caribbean and Asia. This made my guilt return.

Scattered throughout that apartment were literally hundreds of photos – mostly of me (dance recitals, school portraits, birthday parties) -- and some of her. Yet even here there was a sadness, as the photos which featured me were beautifully framed and well organized, while the ones of her were ripped and yellowed. One can see the deterioration of her health in these photos: the reddish skin and jaundiced eyes, the seeming inability to smile, with the exception of those taken at my birthday parties. The record of these photos is a record of her scant happiness – with me. How could I not feel guilty once again?

I found birthday cards given to her in the 1990's, and a Mother's Day card I'd made for her in the 5th grade, 20 years ago. In many of my cards I'd encouraged her to do better, referring to her addictions and health. In some of them I thanked her for loving me unconditionally, for good or bad, as I'd never felt judge by her or that I had to meet any standards of her own choosing.

My guilt returned with a passion when I went through her closets. Her clothes were simple and extra-large. Yet I'd always had nice clothing and was never overweight like my mom. She loved the my clothes and the shape of my body; this made me think all the more of how sad her life must have been. We'd always known it, of course, and tried our best to help. But her addictions were too much for her, I guess, and she just didn't have the personal constitution to fight them. Unsurprisingly, I found Bibles throughout her apartment. I knew she'd always been a believer, searching for something greater than the world offered.

On one wall, there hung a small, wooden plaque. It features a bird soaring into the blue sky, accompanied with the words "Follow Your Dreams." It's not something I'd buy for myself, certainly, but I'd noticed it in the same place for the past 15 years, and grown rather fond of it. I don't know where she got it or who gave it to her, but I took it home and placed it in a beautiful frame. I can't help but think it was meant for me.

CHEREE ALEXANDER-VELEZ (JERENI-SOL)
Bronx Pride

Bodega on every corner & each one a had cat.
Candy up at the front & soda down at the back,
Top Pop soda for 50 cent, snickers & cracker jack,
Cherry ices, bazooka gum and Little Debbie snacks.

We got the Bx 1 bus; you know how we ride,
We got that what? Bronx Pride!

We used to zig zag, play tag and basketball.
Ride bikes and play two hand touch football.
Used to go to the movies 161 mall.
Memories as a kid -man I had ball.

We got the Bx 2 bus; you know how we ride,
We got that what? Bronx Pride.

I'm a Bronx native,
so, I'm naturally creative.
Alumni from Lehman college, so I'm Bronx educated.
Our artists are unique, we can't be replicated.

Cheree Alexander-Velez

I'm from the south Bronx, the south south Bronx where rap
originated.
We are gems in the Bronx, we can be never jaded.

We got the D & B trains; you know how we ride.
We got that what? Bronx Pride.

Now, there's Jenny from the block.
Well, I'm Jereni from the block.
I'm the performing on poet's corner -up & down the writer's
block.
Bronx artists, we prosper and grow,
make you want to "lean back' like Fat Joe.
"It's so hard" like Big Pun to find a "Mona Lisa" without an
afro, braids, & some Adidas sneakers.

We got the 4, 5 & 6 trains; you know how we ride.
We got that what? Bronx pride!

You may know 161st or Kingsbridge Road,
Tremont, Bedford Park, and even Fordham Road,
Just know that, no matter where I go,
that the boogie down Bronx will always be my home.

GLADYSS E. CUEVAS
Heart of gold

If your love is not growing

it is diminishing.

Move on.

As it is not good for one lover to take anything against the
will of

another;

Like your peace.

Gladyss E. Cuevas

Corazón de oro

Si tu amor no está creciendo

Se está desapareciendo.

Sigue tu camino

No es justo que un amante coja cualquier cosa contra la voluntad del

otro;

Como tu paz.

Gladyss E. Cuevas

Moon Child

And at the end of it all there it was

Just me

Staring at the stars, hoping for the moon to make an appearance

Because that is the only time I felt at peace

Releasing the tension in my body

Taking in every energy rotating around me

Breath

Gladyss E. Cuevas

DOLORES NAZARIO-RAMIREZ

Walk with Me

Streets filled

Slick black hair

All turn to look at me

Beige heels walking straight

Golden hoops side to side

Black suit, a dash of red

I got this in the bag

Gladyss E. Cuevas

5 A.M.

Café con pan

Sweet and warm

for when the mornings are cold

For when your eyes are droopy

as you envision your dreams

Café con pan

taste of home

All the love and laughs

you left behind

But don't you worry

A village is here

Café con pan by your side

JESS MARTINEZ

The Old Building on Valentine Avenue

"GOING OUT OF BUSINESS! EVERYTHING MUST GO!" the large yellow banners stated, a few spread out across the old building you could hardly make out the entrance. I hesitated going
inside since I was already running a little later than I wanted to with my errands, but I also knew
it would probably be the last time I would see the inside of the building.

"*Hola, hola, hola mi amiga,*" an older Hispanic man said greeting me from a stool. "*Mi amiga, tenga, tenga,*" he said, and shoved a bunch of flyers in my hand. It had been years since I had stepped inside the large department store, and I was startled to see a furniture store in front of me. There was also what resembled a jewelry shop in the corner; what remained of the clothing
store was up the stairs.

"*Err-ee-thing mast go!*" the Old Man yelled to the sidewalk, which was deserted on the frigid winter day. He shuddered and cranked up the little radiator next to him.

I took my time going up the stairs and stared up at the tall, elegant ceiling, shaped like a dome. Built in 1921, the former synagogue has long been one of my favorite buildings. I was relieved to see that it had been kept mostly intact. The ceiling had newly been painted; gold traced the rim to show off the architecture that dominated The Bronx way back when. The massive window facing the street, although neglected and filthy, beamed light into store, and I couldn't help but remember being a child in the early nineties. I would sit on the second floor stairs and just stare up at the windows passing time, while my mother would elbow other mothers over back-to-school clothes in the background. Most kids would run around, play tag, hide inside the clothing racks, and get scolded by the salespeople. Some would just wait outside on the sidewalk, where older kids would keep an eye out while they blasted music on the portable radios. But I would just sit and stare straight up, daydreaming.

"Jessi, come here," my mom tells me impatiently, waiving a few baby blue button-up school shirts. Her belly is still there, despite that she gave birth three months ago. My sister screams from inside her stroller, hungry, agitated by all of the commotion and unbearable heat. Oh, I'll never forget that heat. The kind that stands still, surrounds and suffocates

you. A large fan in the corner provides no relief to the overcrowded store.

I slowly pick myself up from the floor and drag myself over, with the annoyance of a small child who has been at a clothing store for over ten minutes. *"I don't want the blue ones,"* I tell her as soon as I see the shirts.

"Oh, stop it. They're pretty, you didn't even look!"

"Mami, can we go, are we done, it's too hot in here, I can't sit here anymore, Mami, PLEASE."

"This one has a cute collar. Don't you like the shape of the collar?"

I stare at her like she's crazy. *"I want the yellow shirts again."*

"I told you already," she says trying to control her temper in front of the other mothers, *"Yellow is only for kindergarten. Blue is for first graders and everyone else."*

"You mean blue AND white. Why can't you get the white ones?"

"They ran out of your size. Come here. I need to see if these will last at least until Christmas, knowing you."

I look around the other moms clutching their finds. *"She found some white shirts. And so did she. And so did she."*

"Jessi, I'm not going to ask you again."

"I said NO, Mami," I shriek back and begin to walk away, when I feel a hand grip my arm and yank me backwards.

Ever since my sister was born, I had become unbearable. My quiet and well-mannered self had been replaced with unpredictable whining and tantrums. My mother, twenty-seven years old at the time, had been raised in a culture where a child, especially a younger one, would never think of talking back. She had had it with me. I felt everyone stare as she lost her temper and forced the shirts over my summer dress, right there, in the middle of the store.

"Enough with this bullshit," she says, hissing. *"You're going to wear these shirts and that's that, do you hear me? Chamaquita grosera."*

I hated the fabric, which stuck to my sticky body. I hated my sister, for her constant wailing. And I hated my mom, for becoming That Mother.

She took some money out of her purse and pointed towards the register. *"It's exact change, get in line while I look around. Make sure you get a receipt."*

I stood holding the shirts and the money and watched as she walked towards the baby section with the stroller, the screaming from inside the stroller fading away. The school blouses and baby supplies were nowhere in sight. All that seemed to be left were gym clothes and nightgowns.

"Do you have shorts in a size small?" I asked a bored cashier on her phone. She gestured towards the floor and shook her head.

"Nada, Mamma. That's it."

I browsed through a rack of joggers when she called out, "Buy one, get two free!"

"Why two!" I called back.

"We close this weekend, tryna get rid of everything."

"Do you know what's going to happen to the building?"

"Quién sabe," she replied, shrugging. "Whoever bought it has they hands full, that's all I know."

A few minutes later I settled on a few tank tops and handed over my credit card.

"Cash only," the Cashier said, irritated.

"Is there an ATM?"

"There's a Chase bank on Fordham. Want me to hold them for you?"

"Sure," I reluctantly told her, knowing that I wouldn't be coming back. "Thanks."

"We close in an hour," she said and went back to her phone.

I looked up at the ceiling as I stood on the steps and then at the window. It was cloudy and had started to flurry. I took out my phone and quickly snapped a picture, when I noticed I had received a text from my mother. I ignored it and headed out, and continued my errands.

STEPHANIE RODRIGUEZ
When Love is Light

When winter has overstayed its visit
And the sun tiptoes out of hiding,
Its light appears in segments;
Gold hues, saturate
the bodega gate
the daffodils growing on the edges,
of the botanica
Orange and yellow,
weld onto my skin,
Exposing the freckles dancing on my cheek bones
Kissing my eyelids-
I look down and smile
I see you enter from behind the flowing,
white cortinas in my kitchen
Like a long awaited friend
Warming the brown lipstick stain on my coffee mug
Building mosaics with the colors in my eyes
Even when I know I shouldn't stare too long
You make art out of me regardless
Choosing me for photosynthesis
Without asking for chlorophyll in return

Stephanie Rodriguez

That is how her smile

comforts me

Stephanie Rodriguez

A Homie and a Lover

Raw cacao for your eyes

A soft valley for the curve of your back

A ripe nectarine for your Adam's apple

Cinnamon and molasses for your skin

I'd taste,

Notes of lavender and sage in your thoughts

I remember how

Your laugh would embrace my face like a veil of sunflowers

We don't speak anymore

But how blessed was I to know

Such a wonder.

Stephanie Rodriguez

Remember?

But I am sure I have known you in another life. The
mudslides in your eyes compose memories synonymous with
the gods we used to be.

Remember?

When the light from your body went ablaze against mine,
The world would confuse it for auroras
Our love was the source of illumination-
That dim, subtle street light in the darkest part of the barrio
Hovering above a random act of kindness
Something everyone spoke about.
This past eclipse served as a reminder.
The eyes of the earth looked up
And saw the sun and the moon reenact our
love,
Love.

Joseph Vazquez

JOSEPH VAZQUEZ
February 5, 1999

I rode the BX 27 bus to school like I did every day
But this day was not the same as other days.
I felt tension within as I rode the bus down Westchester Ave
as we approached Wheeler Ave.
I looked intently out the window observing where it all took
place, 41 shots, 19 hits.

I don't know what I was expecting to see,
Residue of a broken spirit?
Pieces of broken hearts mixed with bullet shells on the
sidewalk?

I didn't know Amadou, but this was close to home,
killed by police of the 43rd,
the precinct of my neighborhood.
Something changed in me after that incident. I was too young
when it was Rodney King
but it got a little closer with Abner Louima.

At school, teachers and staff talked about a rally at the
precinct, informing us what to do if we got arrested.

I didn't go to the rally as I struggled with the path I was on.
I was running the streets, pondering change,
stuck in my ways.
Then the change came, I found my voice and had something
to say. I slowly began to take every opportunity to speak out
against injustice.
"Not even 41 shots or 19 hits, a hundred punches and kicks,
plungers and spit, can hold us down, stand your ground!"

Then next year came and it happened again in the same area.
Another young black male killed by the police, but this time
the face was familiar.
I had seen Malcolm playing ball all the time at the Boys and
Girls Club, even played a couple games together.

These were critical times, critical moments
No social media to post and leave quotes in
The only life insurance were words spoken
Voice over silence was vital when their justice was
straight violence

The shaping of a young man's inner-city worldview,
Many couldn't see our inner-city world's point of view.
Kids next town over couldn't even see our truth,

Until we started to take on the root

Stereotypes being portrayed in the news.
A report of a young white male perpetrator showing how well
he did in school,
How he has all the tools.
Another report, a Latino young male perpetrator shows how
he just acts a fool,
Criminal charges, he has more than a few
Portraying lies like crime is on the rise,
We all criminals in their eyes
Further itching the trigger finger itching of those itching to
disfigure figures
That meet a so-called description.

Officials invest in prisons based off the news they listen
Misconception, manipulation, deception,
It's all the same itching like the psychological lynching of
Willie's Lynching
That brought forth a mental prison.

We protested juvenile detention centers that ran like prisons
Had horrible conditions…Spofford

Joseph Vazquez

Went to benefit concerts for political prisoners...Mumia

That's how I found my activism

Now I spread that vision to the youth, that's my mission!

EVELYN PEREZ
4:12 a.m.

Guitar is so hard to hear

Every time a string squeaks in between notes and I see

hands that don't look like yours play

It pulls my feelings from down deep in me

Up to my eyes and everything becomes so hard to see

Deafened and blinded by my memories

Of watching your fingers move

I'm always looking for doppelgängers

of your hands on a guitar

I haven't found them yet

Your hands

Never hurt me

Sometimes they resisted me

But they often relented and pulled me close in the night

Sometimes they needed mine

Sometimes they needed to explore inside

Sometimes they read the braille of my skin

And read me right

Sometimes they trembled brushing the hair from my eyes

As if they were unsure they'd be gentle

Sometimes they grabbed me in all the right ways

Evelyn Perez

Sometimes they'd forget
They are familiar
I still remember
I miss them

LEAH V
Doncellas

All of the maids in Manhattan siamese twinned together and
robotically moving in unison-
doncellas like rockettes kicking dust and dead socks up-
all those merry maids on the move
ducking and weaving through recently renovated linoleums
all those thick tongued so they stay silent unless they're back
on the block ladies--
the ones in plain sight who hide from ridiculous rights!

All them fuck-a-mr-cleaner this be ms-conspicuous!
Spotless Goddess- those warriors never stamped who hardly
stand a chance

The women sealed in sacrifice in order to well-round our
existence, I swear only they compare--

Put my sister, my mother and me in an untouched library
laced with lice
traces of mice
soiled ties
stained rye

oversized dust hidden in
undersized rust the
whole room sus! Just
watch how we navigate that war!

Watch the divinity of fabuloso all over crooks and crevices,
miraculous miracles as unmesses!
Watch the gleam team reign supreme on the pledge floor
scheme!
Watch how Tito Puente moves Mami into magician mode as
she decodes furniture!
Creates center pieces of broken wreaths, grandiose displays
with paperclips and papers dipped in scraps of used
notebooks!
Watch her arrange too many instruments into exhibits she
knows will pivot in palms as she salsas all over my father all
over Willie Colon!
She never misses a beat!
Suddenly the most convoluted space makes neat, she sees
things crowd and creates crowns,
puts it down with the cluster
Now watch while we shift to my sister as she musters, all
things suddenly luster singing Selena
as she thrusts dust into bluster.

Leah V

She's got pollo marinating, washing clothes while cooking,
spitting Biggie while hooking pots to their places making
space in all napes
And Amy serenades me as I move mountains to mop tops.
We're all prancing
Making backdrops
Debating articles & recalling chronicles of when we had less.
When it was busses and frozen meals 'cause Mami worked
overtime, because Aitza made two more human-kinds
We been trained as caregivers, soldiers of servitude
I swear my mother will suggest the shirt off her back after
forcing upon you a baked goods attack! I've seen my sister
take out the last of what she had and place it on my plate and
yelled 'eat it' in my face!

This keeping-of-house makes me reflect, makes me depict
my ancestors calloused corroded and singing sweetness,
cutting sweet sticks along the island all the same.
When they stared out into the sea, colonized by Spain
followed by good ol' American Joe,
when the sand between their toes felt less free than it had
before,
when they struggled with sounds of uncertain closed-curtain
illogical ingles,

when they began to change the way they dressed,

when they didn't realize as citizens they remained oppressed,

when they were sexualized and used,

labeled stupid yet pursued,

when San Juan became the Bronx,

when the back door became the front

had they ever imagined, did they ever think

It could be our floors we scrubbed!

Our very own tiles rubbed!

Rubbing past the foreign falsified identity of Mrs Liberty

wearing uggs, passed the D train toward us.

We hold magic!

Anything you can do we can do bleeding!

Anything you can do we can do beating eggs for entire

elaborate guest lists of our own meetings.

The men make space for us in our era. En nuestra familia the

patriarchy moves aside the wage gap and cares for us even if

we can't move aside our pride to ask.

My father worships the woman he wed. They act as a unit so

fluid that I've learned to not tell one without expecting the

other to address the cover with me directly!

The roles we hold reek of respect, we never neglect the needs

of one another because we know we're stronger together than

alone and fighting white America as a whole been the goal-since 18 we brought it to the polls!

And we brought it to the other poles, the ones that hold

palms as we walk up stairs-

'Mira Leah don't forget that spot over there' my mother

reminds me.

We been cleaning! It's in our blood to scrub!

Called me a spic & I scrubbed that,

compared me to Sofia Vergara & I scrubbed that!

My tongue contains multitudes, my linguistic skill is

overused- I does that.

Gonzalez women hit you with the

EnglishSpanishSpanglishEbonicsLatinRoot all while hovering

over hot food! We bounce back.

We cater, we carry, we clean, we never concede, we attack,

eloquently.

It's best you bless yourself by seeing us out of that box before

we break out.

We've got numbers-

largest growing population in New York City.

So build your walls & our Lysol disinfectant wipes will ruin

by rubbing you off and then we'll walk down collegiate aisles

all smiles all educated and dedicated to our people!

But what do I know?

I'm just a Nuyorican chick on all fours on the floor answering
my Saint Mother's call not being able to recall the last time I
mopped that corner of the hallway.
We've got magic, we stem from soil.
My mother the sun, my sister the water. Now watch us make
corruption weep, watch us seep into society, watch me
blossom into my ancestors wildest dreams.
"Que bonita bandera"
we sing while we clean, clean, clean.

JENNIFER AROCHA
hello, goodbye

it was that meaningless goodbye.
that I'll miss you,
turning into one more night goodbye.
it was that goodbye
where you and I both knew
you're still mine.
and,
something inside
knew we would still try.
it was that goodbye,
where our bodies intertwined,
the one that still led you
in between my thighs
where the sight of my nakedness
made you mesmerize,
still capturing your eyes.
it was that
we didn't really mean it, goodbye
the one I'll never forget
where you will always come back
after all the times you've left.

Jennifer Arocha

that goodbye where
where it's always a hello,
it was that goodbye,
where we never really let go.
goodbye, again.

REBEKAH LOVE
Nora

E found a way to move Nora's waist even closer to his as the next song filled the bathroom with thick sexual energy.

Your hands on my hips pull me right back to you
I catch that thrust, give it right back to you
You're in so deep, I'm breathing for you
You grab my braids, arch my back high for you

Nora felt an electrical current run from her pelvic, to her waist, which then traveled through E's hands. She felt the current run through her body into his, then back. They were transferring energy specifically, Nora's heightened energy. E ran his hands up and down her waist, landing on her hips, gently squeezing them.

"This feels better than I remember".
She didn't mean to, but she busted out laughing, lifting her head, turning to face him.

"Yeah, this is definitely better than before".
She wrapped her arms around his waist, her head slightly aback. She stared at her second-best decision post college. It was happening as Nora realized it was happening. An intense and warm sensation came over her body, familiar, sensual,

and electric. She noticed E's pupils dilate as she felt an urge to be inside of him. She watched him experience what she's been exploring behind the shower curtain all week. His lips were slightly ajar as if to speak but to be careful with his words. He chose no words and instead leaned forward to kiss her lips.
You're diesel engine, I'm squirting mad oil
All down on the floor 'til my speaker starts to boil

E's hands continued to run up and down her waist, momentarily stopping to squeeze it. She felt a current which lengthen her posture, the sensation straitening her back. She stood taller on her big toes, pushing forward for a deeper kiss. They were swaying back and fourth, to the music, their own beat, and the electric energy traveling between them. Nora's arms slid up his back, her hands landing at the base of his neck. She felt him feel his neck hairs stand up. He noticed this moment, pausing to acknowledge that he felt her feel him. With his right hand on her cheek, he stared into her eyes, momentarily searching for understanding. He was so turned on by their new connection but also complacent with the unknown of their new connection, E leaned forward kissing his partner more passionately. He wrapped his arms around her back pulling her closer, slightly lifting her frame off the tub floor. What ensued in a tug of war, E and Nora pulled, squeezed, and rubbed against one another, each movement igniting raw pleasure. Pleasure moved in and out of every hole on Nora's body and into E's. She was welcomed into his pleasure world as her body embraced him into hers as and Jill Scott's lyrics fueling their fire.

I flip shit, quick slip, hip dip and I'm twisted
In your hands and your lips and your tongue tricks
And you're so thick and you're so thick and you're so
And you're so...

It was as if her voice empowered Nora's heightened abilities feeding into their sexual chemistry. Similarly, to the way Nora's body responded to the essential oils that night, their properties intensifying her powered senses, Nora and E's elevated shared energy was intensified by the sounds from the speaker. With the right amount of aggression and gentleness, E pushed Nora against the shower's wall pressing his body against hers. Then, slightly bending his knees to lift her up. What came after was the clapping sound of Nora's wet back against the tiled wall. E began to move to the instruments of D'Angelo's Crusin' as the melody filled the room.

We're gonna fly away, plan to go my way
I love it when we're cruising together

E grabbed Nora's thighs holding her up and grounding himself. The cooling effect of the tile balanced the hot beads of water crashing onto E's back. Nora held onto his shoulders for support basking in the cool sensation of the tile on her skin and the steam from the hot water.

Music was made for love, cruising is made for love
I love it when we're cruising together

E's body moved to the tempo of D'Angelo's voice as his waist vibrated from his slow movements while holding up Nora's body.

Baby tonight belongs to us
Everything's right, do what you must
And inch by inch we get closer and closer oh
Every little part is in touch

Their shower phased out not with a climax but more kissing, rubbing, and squeezing. E slowly let Nora onto her feet as she breathed into his neck, taking in his naturally sweet body odor. She breathed what seemed like his essence as she settled onto her feet. E was still holding her waist as he turned off the shower head. The sound of the knob turning off pierced E and Nora's ears. His head jerked back a bit, not at the sound but the sudden realization that there *was* something happening here.

He turned to Nora and asked, "tell me I'm not bugging, did you hear that?"

"Yes babe, I heard it".

Surprisingly, Nora was not as thrilled to share in on this experience as E was. She felt exposed but mostly protective of her new 'powers'.

"What *was* that?" "I mean I know it was the water, but I feel like it was so much louder, like I heard the water inside of my ear. Did you hear it the same?" "Damn, I feel crazy, am I even making sense?"

Nora reached for E's towel passing it to him then reached for her's wrapping her body as she stepped out of the tub.

"Yes babe, you're making sense".

With one hand holding his towel, E reached out and gently grabbed Nora's elbow.

"Hey, what's going on?" "You've been distant for weeks?" "I can't allow you to escape this conversation, Nora I feel..."

E paused, hesitating, almost regretful about what he was about to say.

"Nee, I know what you're thinking"

Nora slowly looked at E.

I know

His eyes widened and he almost jumped out of his skin.

"Oh shit, my nigga do you know what this *means*?"

E could not contain his excitement which made Nora excited.

"What babe, what does it mean?" Nora smirked at her man, not surprised at all about his joy.

She realized when he turned off the water that his superpowers were activated by their experience and she knew he could read her mind.

"I can *read your mind* Nee"

A natural introvert, Nora's indifference was overshadowed by E's excitement. They were experiencing two sides of the same coin. Nora was still getting to know herself and this felt like the perfect opportunity to do it alone. Although she loved her partner, she felt prematurely exposed, forced to share a coming of age moment. She also felt bittersweet about E's ability to read her mind. She could not read his mind but he could hear what she was saying to herself. Her thoughts will be the last bit of privacy she's known.

E calmed himself, to Nora's assumption, to read her mind. She rolled her eyes turning her back to him, maybe if she didn't face him, he couldn't get to what no person has no right to.

"I understand how you feel. I'm excited, I'm sorry I can't help it. But I understand how invasive this is".

"Yeah babe, it is"

"So, can we talk about it? Please? This shit is crazy, we on some X-Men shit"

She turned back around and laughed.

"That's exactly what I thought when it first happened to me"

"Oh so, you can read my mind too"? he asked.

"No, no. I have different...powers. I can feel, my senses are on ten. I'm like Daredevil without the blindness".

"Nee that's amazing. How long have you been...like Daredevil?"

Nora couldn't help but smile. E was the outwardly curious one and desperate to understand everything that excited him.

"About a week".

"A week, really?"

His curiosity was peeked but only slightly drowned by his disappointment that she kept *this* from him.

"Yeah, I was going to tell you eventually. I just wanted time to understand it".

"Eventually like a few months from now?"

Nora smiled. He was not wrong. Nora was the opposite from E in her way of understanding things which was were through thinking about them alone. E was the only student who enjoyed group projects while Nora always found a way to work solo.

"Yeah eventually E, you know me. I just needed some time to myself. I still need time to myself. Can we get dressed though? "Why are we still in here?"

E paused looking down realizing that he was drying but still wet and naked.

He smirked looking at her.

"You still got another one in you".

She laughed again. "Can we just put some clothes on".

"Anything you want babe".

Thank You San Juan

I'm sitting on the balcony of our San Juan Airbnb. It is 4 o'clock in the morning and I'm procrastinating. But I feel good about it because it's void of guilt. I'm actually acknowledging without the toxic guilt trip, such an unnecessary and nasty feeling. I know it so well, I live guilt, breathe it, speak it, and use it.

But here I am happily trailing off from completing an assignment due at midnight. In hindsight, I've written more towards this assignment in the past 3 hours, then I have back home. My thoughts, ideas, and focus are all working together, formulating the words I need to complete my work.

The music in my beats headphones is from my Chill playlist. It feels incredible to just be and be productive. Man, how difficult it is to create that space in New York.

I love New York but Thank You San Juan.

Thank you for giving me black girl magic, skin glowin', man resting, self-loving; vacation poppin', singing like no one's listening, Tumblr scrolling, balcony series.

EDITOR ACKNOWLEDGEMENTS

First and foremost, thank you to all the skilled writers that contributed and submitted to the first BX Writers Anthology. You all kept me inspired and motivated to see this book through. Your diverse storytelling and New York City centric poetry has made this Anthology what it is today; a book by the people, for the people. This is only the first of many books/projects to come. Thank you to my partner Amaurys Grullon for all the work and love that you've poured into The Bronx. Special shoutout to Anabel Encarnación for creating a perfect introduction and always providing me with great ideas since day one of BX Writers. And of course, thank you to my mom and family, for always instilling in me to love, work hard, and to give back to others. Te amo.

BIOGRAPHIES

JOSUE CACERES

Josué Caceres, author of Out of Place and Bronx Stories & Heartbreak, is a creative born and raised in the South Bronx. Since young he had expressed a liking for writing poetry. In his work he explores themes around relationships, identity, and toxic masculinity. Through his poetry he hopes to shed light on the particular experiences he's had growing up in the Bronx and coming from a Dominican decent. He is currently the brand manager of Bronx Native and founder of BX Writers.

BX WRITERS

BX Writers is a platform under Bronx Native that Josué started in February 2018. His main goal with BX Writers is to highlight and showcase writers from his community. He believes that representation is important and that those in his community have a story to tell. BX Writers has hosted open mics, poetry events, book clubs, and workshops. This is the first BX Writers Anthology.

AMAURYS GRULLON

Amaurys Grullon is a creative & entrepreneur based in The South Bronx. He is the co-founder and CEO of Bronx Native.

BRONX NATIVE

A brand that embodies what The Bronx truly is. Highlighting The Bronx through art, media, apparel, events and more. Changing the narrative and showcasing what The BX excellence.

RESOURCES

Josué Caceres
Instagram- @josue_caceres
Email- josue@bronxnative.com

BX Writers
Instagram- @bxwriters
Facebook- BX Writers
Email- josue@bronxnative.com

Amaurys Grullon
Website- amaurysgrullon.com
Email- amaurysgrullon@gmail.com
Social Media- @amaurysgrullon

Bronx Native
Instagram- @thebronxnative
Facebook- The Bronx Native
Twitter- @bxnative
127 Lincoln Ave Bronx, NY

Made in the USA
Las Vegas, NV
23 January 2023

66162909R00184